OURAY HIKING GUIDE

FAVORITE HIKING TRAILS OF OURAY, COLORADO

KELVIN B. KENT

Ridgway, Colorado

PUBLISHED BY WAYFINDER PRESS
P. O. BOX 217
RIDGWAY, COLORADO 81432
PUBLISHER: MARCUS WILSON

PRINTED BY COUNTRY GRAPHICS,
RIDGWAY, COLORADO

PHOTOS: KELVIN B. KENT

FRONT COVER:
The final stretch to the top of Mt. Sneffels —
Kit Moore, Eli Moore and Kelvin Kent.
Photo by Larry Lindsay

BACK COVER:
Kelvin Kent, with his wife Becky Lindsay and
Black Lab, Angie taken on an overnight trip near
Hunchback Mountain.

ISBN 0-943727-15-4

THANKS AND APPRECIATION

This guide is for all hikers, young and old, who enjoy and respect the pleasure of getting out on foot into the mountains.

In particular I dedicate the following pages to my wife Becky, who not only has been my constant hiking companion on all of these trails over the last few years, but has also shown and taught me much about the beautiful San Juan Mountains and has encouraged me to pursue the idea of actually producing this guide so that others may more readily share the opportunity to enjoy what God has made for all of us.

Thanks, too, to my daughter Melanie, for helping to type and decipher my writing, and for joining us on several of our outings. And to Peter, my son, who has been supportive of the effort but thinks my timings are outrageously slow and has not yet discovered that resting and taking in the view, is part of the experience!

And not forgetting one more companion who covers at least three times the distance as we do on all of our hikes: our Black Lab Angie, who has left her mark everywhere!

And lastly, my thanks, appreciation, and respect for those who have gone before me and have helped provide insight, information, inspiration and the type of first hand knowledge that will soon die if not passed on. I refer here to older Ouray residents like Roger and Angie Henn, George and Bernice Swift, Ruth Miller, Bill Forsythe and others.

May our hiking in the mountains of Ouray provide more than merely exercise!

CONTENTS

Ouray Hiking Guide

Favorite Hiking Trails of Ouray, Colorado

PURPOSE

This book has been written in an attempt to answer the many questions and frustrations encountered over the past few years when talking to fellow hikers on the trail or to those who are trying vainly to find a trailhead or get information which may help them plan their outing.

It, in no way, tries to be in competition with other publications such as the very useful *Hiking Trails of Ouray County*, but it does seek to offer a different perspective in what is hoped to be a practical, simple, and easy-to-follow method of seeing what a hike consists of and achieving it without getting lost!

By keeping it simple and non-technical, maps, although desirable, are not essential and none of the hikes or walks selected need special equipment, although a compass is always desirable.

Many locals and experienced hikers of the area will already be familiar with the hikes described, but for those visiting our beautiful town of Ouray and its surrounding mountains, I do hope that this will enable you to enjoy the area better and explore some of the greatest scenery in the country, if not the world!

Although this book is written and published for the enjoyment of all who use it, care should be taken to observe private property notices and not violate the rights of property owners over whose land a trail or access road may pass.

There are bound to be discrepancies here and there and any constructive criticism, suggestions or corrections will be most gratefully received and can be directed to Kelvin Kent, 1144 Ridge, Montrose, Colorado 81401.

"It is intended that a portion of any profits made by the sale of this book be donated to the Ouray Mountain Rescue and local Trail Maintenance Organizations." Kelvin B. Kent

1

A REQUEST

If there would be one object in mind, here, it would be for all of us to enjoy our hiking. Part of this enjoyment comes from being prepared and knowing beforehand what is involved. I would like therefore to strongly request that the following be read responsibly and not just be glossed over as a formality. Thanks a lot.

DEGREES OF DIFFICULTY

In assessing the degrees of difficulty listed on page 6 (Trails Summary), the following factors have been taken into account:
Length of hike
Elevation at the top
Exposure to elements
State of the trail or route
Proximity to roads and rescue facilities
Physical effort required
Steepness
Total time required
No trail requires ropes, technical climbing skill or special equipment. However, keep in mind that what may be considered easy or moderate for an athletic teenager may be very difficult for some adults or even for visitors who are not fully acclimated. I know people of five and seventy-five who have been to the top of Mount Sneffels and many in their thirties who haven't made it. The object of grading the degree of difficulty is to put the various trails into categories so that the reader and hiker have a better idea of what level to attempt. Remember, bad weather conditions or inadequate clothing can turn a moderate hike into a more-than-difficult hike.

GUIDING RULES & SUGGESTIONS

1. Footwear is important; hiking boots recommended.
2. Water, however delicious, may not be safe to drink.
3. Take plenty of water. (Ideally 1 quart per person.)
4. Let someone know where you are going and what time you expect to be back. Carry some form of identification.
5. Part of the beauty of these trails is their cleanliness. Please haul out what you take in.
6. Weather conditions can change rapidly. Be prepared.
7. Summer sun, especially at these elevations can be dangerous. Watch exposure and use sun screen.
8. At certain times, insects (flies and mosquitoes) can be bad. Take insect repellent.
9. On trails which are foot and horse, remember that the horse has the right of way.
10. If you take a dog, you should have a leash ready to use if necessary.
11. If possible take a book on wildflowers.
12. Timings are based on a slow to moderate "plod" with time for rests and photographs. The total round trip time does allow 45 minutes or so for lunch.
13. The best time of day to go is right after breakfast. It is cooler and the likelihood of showers and rain are less in the morning than afternoon. If thunder is heard, hikers should immediately descend and not stay in the open - especially above timberline.
14. When switchbacks are involved, please DO NOT short-cut them. Some of the terrain is delicate and damage can easily result if care is not taken.
15. Often, trails are marked by a trail blaze sign. It looks like this ☐ and is usually cut into the bark of trees about 8 feet from ☐ the ground.
16. Be sensible in assessing your physical condition. Elevation in these hikes can be dangerous, especially for heart conditions or lack of acclimation.

🚶🚶

TIMES OF YEAR

We generally do our hiking from Memorial Day to early October. Earlier on, even until the end of June or early July, there can still be a fair amount of snow and certain trails are just not feasible for the average hiker. Similarly it is possible to get significant snowfalls from mid September onwards and it is therefore advisable to look for or listen to area weather forecasts. Temperatures, too, can plunge dramatically in a short space of time, especially in the fall season.

Another factor which may influence the choice of a hike is the wild flower season although it is fair to say that any time after the beginning of June provides color, beauty and an innumerable selection of alpine flora. July and August are generally considered the best times for high country flowers such as columbine, delphinium and larkspur, but so many others co-exist and vary with elevation and the direction of the slope that I have never been disappointed. Indeed there is always a beautiful array of vegetation and flowers from June through September.

The last factor to be considered in selecting a hike is Summer heat and angle of the sun.

EARLY SEASON TRAILS

These trails are generally open earlier and remain open later:

Portland Mine
Dexter Creek (June onwards)
Twin Peaks (June onwards)
Weehawken - Alpine Mine Overlook
Oak Creek (June onwards)
Upper Cascade Falls
Corbett Creek
Weehawken Creek
*The Old Turntable - see note
*Guston - see note
Baldy
Bear Creek

4

*Note: The Old Turntable and Guston Trails

In 1994 a large cleanup operation was commenced which will continue through 1997. In addition to implementing measures to improve water quality in the area caused by earlier years of mining activity, there is also a revegetation effort which will greatly improve the looks and ecology.

These hikes pass through some of the cleanup areas and are for the most part on private property. Special care should therefore be taken to understand that any privilege granted at the time is not necessarily automatic and that heavy equipment may be present and prevent access in certain areas. Unsuitable behavior by hikers could result in the closing of this trail, so please be aware and careful.

For the 1996 season, access to these trails may be difficult. The little bridge which crosses the creek to get to the Joker Boarding House at the start of the Old Turntable Trail has been removed. It is not yet clear if this bridge will be replaced.

MID-SEASON TRAILS

These trails are usually fine for mid-season (end of June to early September) but can still have good amounts of snow either side of July and August:

Bridge of Heaven
Blue Lakes
Hayden
Sneffels
Ice Lake
Blaine Basin
Mt. Abrams
Courthouse Mountain

Note: It has occurred to me that because our own hiking of the various trails has been done over the entire hiking season, certain descriptions of flowers, etc. may not be completely accurate for other times of the year.

🚶🚶

TRAIL SUMMARY

Trail Name	Round Trip Time from Downtown Ouray	Degree of Difficulty	High Clearance Vehicle or 4x4
1. The Old Turntable	3 hours	Easy	No (if you wade the stream — otherwise yes
2. Guston Area	3.5 hours	Easy	No
3. Portland Mine	3.5 hours	Moderate	No
4. Weekawken - Alpine Mine	4.5 hours	Moderate	No
5. Weehawken - Weehawken Creek	5 hours	Moderate	No
6. Corbett Creek	4.5 to 6.5 hours	Moderate	No
7. Oak Creek	5 hours	Moderate	No
8. Baldy	4.5 to 5.5 hours	Moderate	No
9. Bear Creek	4 to 6.5 hours	Moderate	No
10. Dexter Creek	7 hours	Moderate	No
11. Blue Lakes	6.5 to 8.5 hours	Moderate/Difficult	No
12. Chief Ouray Mine (Upper Cascade Falls)	4.5 hours	Moderate/Difficult	No
13. Bridge of Heaven	6.5 hours	Difficult	No (but desireable)
14. Twin Peaks	6 hours	Difficult	No
15. Blaine Basin	6 to 7 hours	Difficult	No
16. Ice Lake	8 hours	Difficult	No
17. Courthouse Mountain	6 to 7 hours	Difficult	No
18. Mount Abrams	6 hours	Difficult	No
19. Mount Hayden	6.5 to 7.5 hours	Difficult	Yes
20. Mount Sneffels	6 to 9 hours	Difficult	Yes

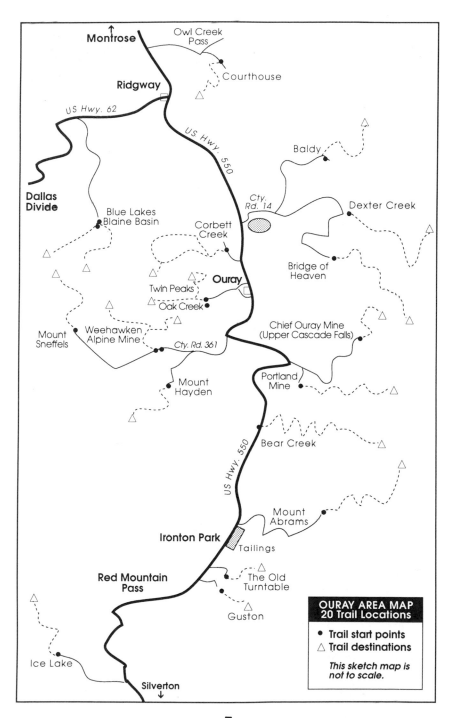

Montrose

Owl Creek Pass

Courthouse

Ridgway

US Hwy. 62

US Hwy. 550

Baldy

Dallas Divide

Cty. Rd. 14

Dexter Creek

Blue Lakes Blaine Basin

Corbett Creek

Bridge of Heaven

Twin Peaks

Ouray

Oak Creek

Chief Ouray Mine (Upper Cascade Falls)

Mount Sneffels

Weehawken Alpine Mine

Cty. Rd. 361

Mount Hayden

Portland Mine

US Hwy. 550

Bear Creek

Mount Abrams

Ironton Park

Tailings

Red Mountain Pass

The Old Turntable

Guston

Ice Lake

Silverton

OURAY AREA MAP
20 Trail Locations

• Trail start points
△ Trail destinations

This sketch map is not to scale.

7

1. THE OLD TURNTABLE

Elevation:	Start at 10,000 feet End at 10,300 feet
Time:	From Ouray to trailhead by car- 15 minutes From trailhead to turntable- 1 hour From turntable to bottom- 30 minutes Allow 2 to 3 hours for round trip (more if you want to explore)
Map:	USGS Topographical Ironton
Difficulty:	Easy *See note on page 5

GENERAL DESCRIPTION

This isn't really a trail so much as a reminiscent journey to the turn of the century to discover the remains of an old railway line and turntable amidst the ruins of mines long since dormant. The trail itself is only about a mile long but one could spend days exploring the wooded countryside close by which is filled with wildflowers, mushrooms, mosses and literally dozens of mines, buildings and legacies of Ouray's heyday.

The main difficulty is finding the trailhead and getting across a 15 foot wide river to get to it. Either 4-wheel drive is needed or strong wading ability! The round trip for the trail itself is a total of 2 miles but could be much more if you'd like to explore.

THE TRAIL

Start Point: The trailhead is 9 miles from Ouray on the Million Dollar Highway towards Red Mountain Pass. Go 6.5 miles south on Highway 550 until the road flattens out and you see an old stone building on the left of the road. Continue for another 1.25 miles on the straight level portion of the highway. See mine tailings on left. Proceed on past a small wood building on the right, up incline to a sign indicating 10,000 feet. Go past this to two 35 MPH signs and on to a 25 MPH sign. Right opposite

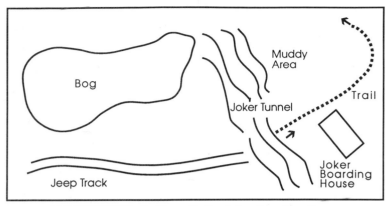

OLD TURNTABLE - Trailhead is the Joker Boarding House

the 25 MPH sign is a small, difficult-to-see, road going off the highway to the left. At this stage look south and see a well-preserved 2-story wood building known as the Joker Boarding House. This is the trailhead. Drive down the small road and cross the river (carefully). At the junction go straight on, not right, and come back up on top of tailings to the 2-story building. Park either side of the muddy stream to the west of the bog area.

As you start, look across to the southeast corner of the bog. This is the old Joker tunnel used to drain water and carry minerals and ore from the mines further up Red Mountain. The Boarding House was built in 1903.

Walk up the trail to the left of the Boarding House and follow the road as it turns sharply left. After about .25 mile come to a junction and keep straight on, not right.

A little further on the trail splits again. Go straight, not right, and a few yards later look for a junction where one road goes down, left; keep straight on the main road. Go around the left side of some small tailings mounds and proceed to the end of what was an old jeep road. You will have come to the large tailings and remains of Paymaster Mine to your front and to the right. At the very end of the road look for a small path going slightly left; this path is a few yards after a small stream bed draining water to the left. You are now following the actual railway line. At this point the trail is fairly level, going back north with beautiful views down to the Ironton Valley and up across the highway left to Richmond Pass and Hayden Mountain. After about 500 yards the trail bears right up towards

9

The Joker Boarding House with trail going up to the left

Red Mountain #2 over a 'bund.' This is a man-made raised area built by the Ute Indian labor for Ouray pioneer Otto Mears who conceived the idea of getting the old Silverton train to come down to serve the mines of this area from the town of Red Mountain. But there was no way for the train to turn around and, therefore, a turntable had to be built to allow the engine (which was always on the down end of the train) to decouple, turn 180 degrees on the manually operated turntable and rejoin the cars, back in its position on the down end.

Very shortly you can see the main line coming in from the right joining the old line you are on. (There may still be a blue diamond sign on a spruce tree on the right side of the trail.) Just ahead is the turntable which was probably last used in 1922 — about 70 years ago.

It is interesting to walk 1/2 mile or so back along the main line to see very good evidence of the old railway track and the way in which the line was built, sometimes by blasting the rock face itself. Mine shafts off to the right are clearly visible.

On the way back, another detour can be taken at the Paymaster Mine junction where an offshoot of the main trail goes down to the right following a winter cross-country ski trail sign. At the bottom of this track are the remains of another huge mine and just to the north of it is the old Silverbelle Mine.

Remember that generally, this is private property.

2. GUSTON AREA

Elevation:	Start 10,274 feet.
	Top 10,900 feet.
Time:	From Ouray to trailhead by car - 17 minutes
	From trailhead to top - 1 hour
	From top to bottom - 45 minutes
	Allow 2.5 to 3 hours for round trip (trail only)
Map:	USGS Topographical Ironton
Difficulty:	Easy *See note on page 5

GENERAL DESCRIPTION

This is another walk which is more historical than anything else. It is not so much an actual hike as it is a visit to Ouray's mining past on Red Mountain. Apart from one creek-crossing which entails a scramble down a bank and up the other side, the trail is really a small road and easy to walk on.

The main features are mines and buildings and outstanding views across the Million Dollar Highway of the west side of the Hayden Mountain group of peaks.

For an outing that is quite different and brings the old mining history of the area dramatically to life, this is a highly interesting and unusual walk which could occupy anything from a short half day to a full day in time — depending on the extent of exploration.

The round trip for the trail itself is about 2 miles.

THE TRAIL

Start Point: The trailhead is 9.7 miles from Ouray going South on the Million Dollar Highway. Drive up Red Mountain, through the flat area of Ironton and, after reaching a signpost indication the 10,000 ft. contour level go past two switchbacks. Just before a third switchback, look for a switchback sign with 15 MPH on it. At this switchback (where there is a double telephone pole on the left) pull over to the left side of the road at the side of a tailings. Park here.

Keeping the tailings on your right, walk westward for 200 yards until creek is reached. At the time of writing, efforts were underway to rebuild an old tressle bridge spanning the creek: cross the newly constructed bridge and continue walking left on the road, making a loop with a smaller stream on your left. After about 15 minutes the road splits. Keep left. In another few minutes, part of the old Guston Mine can be seen to the left.

At the next little junction, go right and head on up the hill until you reach a definite right bend with a smaller, less defined road going into a meadow to the left. Take this left into the meadow and head for a definite rocky outcrop feature. It is this meadow which once housed the community of Guston. It was called Camp Guston and although quite large it was never incorporated as a township.

On reaching the rock feature (known as the Guston Knob) you can see the old Robinson Mine above and to the right. Also notice remains of the old railroad bed where a spur came down from the town of Red Mountain.

Having walked around the knob towards the mountain, cross a small stream and head on up north keeping the mountain on your right. After 100 yards or so look for a small wooden building just above you to the right and make your way towards it up the bank. This building was the covered waiting room for the train.

Just past it (going back south) is the remains of the old railway platform.

Carry on south (following what was the old railway line), with the remains of the old Robinson Mine up to your left, for another 200 yards to a fallen-down structure and small standing building. The fallen structure was the Robinson Mine power house and still contains a huge boiler and windlass machine. Just to the right is one of the old shafts.

This place makes a pleasant rest stop with superb views across the valley and is about 1 hour from the start point.

From here, continue on the old railroad south and cross a fill followed by a cut through a rocky area. Up to the left you can now see the remains of the Genessee/Vanderbilt Mine, while down to the right is the Yankee Girl Mine. Below this, in the bottom of the valley and occupying the space up to the highway is the more modern Idarado Mine Complex.

At this point take the road that keeps on the level and then goes slightly downhill for 200 yards to a junction where four roads meet.

The Yankee Girl Mine

Turn a sharp right and go downhill past the Yankee Girl Mine to the junction where you entered the meadow at Guston. This time, continue on the main road and look for a small aspen stand on the left. Go past this, round a curve and come to a second aspen stand, also on the left. Here take a small detour into the aspen and up the small tree-covered ridge to discover the old Guston Church remains. You can still see the bell tower on the ground and maybe even see the pastors name (Reverend Davis) written on a section of old chimney metal. The story goes that funds ran out for the building of this church and although the bell tower was in place there was no bell. So the miners rigged up a whistle which took its place and was blown by steam produced by the mine! Next to the remains of the church is a sturdy building which was probably the rectory or summer house for the pastor.

From here, return to the main road and walk back to the start point.

3. PORTLAND MINE

Elevation:	Start - 8100 feet
	Top - 9200 feet
	Total distance for round trip - 4.2 miles
Time:	Ouray to start point by car - 4 minutes
	Start point to top - 1.25 hours
	Top to bottom - 1 hour
	Allow 2.5 to 3.5 hours for round-trip
Map:	USGS Topographical Ouray
Difficulty:	Easy

GENERAL DESCRIPTION

This is an easy trail with an elevation gain of only 1100 feet to a high point of 9200 feet. It is comparatively gentle and meanders up through the base of the Amphitheater to the Portland Mine. Vegetation is varied with meadows, spruce, aspen, and pine, and the hike takes less than a half day. Although not a mountain-top experience, there are very pleasant views across the valley and back over Ouray to the Hayden Range and up Canyon Creek towards Camp Bird.

There are actually two different starting points, one from the Amphitheater Campground and the other from the South of Portland Creek on the Portland Road. Both trails meet after about a third of a mile and continue on the one trail.

This trail guide chooses the Portland Road trailhead as the start point and, in my opinion, the most scenic way to go.

THE TRAIL (FOREST SERVICE TRAIL #238)

Drive south out of Ouray on Highway 550 for one mile and turn left just after the second switchback into the Amphitheater Campground road. Note that this road is officially open only during the main season from about mid-May to end of September. If closed, park just before the gate on the left and proceed on foot as follows. If open, drive up the road for about 100 yards and take the gravel road to the right. This road is a little rough

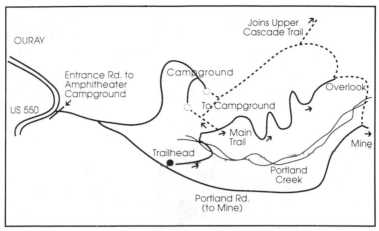

PORTLAND TRAIL -
Links up with Amphitheater Campground and Upper Cascade Trail

and bumpy but the trailhead is only a quarter of a mile up it on the left where there is parking space.

Start by walking to the right of the creek and then cross the creek on a good wooden bridge before proceeding up and away from the creek in a Northwest direction. The trail then turns back to the right into the spruce forest entering a small stand of aspen with the remains of an old log cabin on the right. After about 10 or 15 minutes of hiking a junction is reached. This is the meeting place of the trail coming up from the campground, which in turn leads to another trail going up to Chief Ouray Mine (Upper Cascade Falls). Our path stays on the Portland Trail which leads to an overlook after 1.5 miles.

The trail now winds uphill through a series of gentle switchbacks offering glimpses of the peaks to the west through the trees. After about 35 minutes or so the trail opens to the south with views of the operating Grizzly Bear Connection Mine on the opposite hillside.

Now the trail continues to rise slowly, moving deeper into the heart of the Amphitheater. After another 10 minutes or so it opens out at a scenic overlook with expansive views of the Amphitheater walls above and a good perspective of Mount Hayden to the southwest.

Here, we have three options. One can either stop, to enjoy

Portland Creek from the Overlook
(Amphitheater walls in background -
Portland Mine up to the right)

the views and turn around to return the same way or go on another few feet to a junction where you can turn right and, after about half a mile, meet up with the Portland Mine road. This road returns to the trailhead and is an easy walk but it does, from time to time, have heavy traffic, dirt bikes, and other vehicles on it. The third option is to take the trail going left at the junction which is still marked Portland trail and proceed west for a half mile through wooded hillside, crossing a usually dry creek and back up to a point where it meets the Upper Cascade (Chief Ouray Mine) trail. If you do this, you can again either turn around and go back the same way or turn left and descend on the Cascade Trail for about 1.3 miles to another junction which points back to meet the main Portland Mine Trail just above the wooden bridge. As you descend you will also see a turn off to the right leading back to the campground but keep straight ahead to come out at the start point. Reading this, it may appear a little complicated but this trail (and its other options) are very clearly marked and there is little chance of getting lost!

4. WEEHAWKEN/ALPINE MINE

Elevation:	Start 8700 feet
	End of trail at overlook 10,900 feet
Time:	Ouray to start point - 8 minutes (by car)
	Start to junction of Weehawken/Alpine
	Mines Trails - 1 hour
	Junction to Alpine Mine overlook - 1 hour
	Return - 1.5 hours
	Total round trip - allow 4.5 hours
Map:	USGS Topographical Ouray and Ironton
Difficulty:	Moderate

GENERAL DESCRIPTION

This trail is called the Weehawken trail and shares the same initial one hour climb to an obvious junction point where the old Weehawken Trail continues up the valley and this trail bears to the right. It is a great trail for generally limbering up. It offers varied terrain, beautiful views of Mt. Hayden, lovely aspen glades and, from the overlook, an unparalleled view of Ouray and a vista embracing the Cimarron Mountain Range all the way around to Imogene Pass. It is not difficult and measures just over 2.5 miles to the top. There is no water source at all on this trail.

THE TRAIL

Start Point: 2.7 miles up the Camp Bird Mine Road on the right. Go south from Ouray on Highway 550 and turn right after the first switchback on County Road 361 which goes to Camp Bird and Yankee Boy Basin. After 2 miles cross a bridge and proceed another .7 mile. Look for small opening on the right with Weehawken Trail sign. There is parking space here for about 4 vehicles with more space on the opposite side of the road.

Proceed up this very well maintained trail through a series

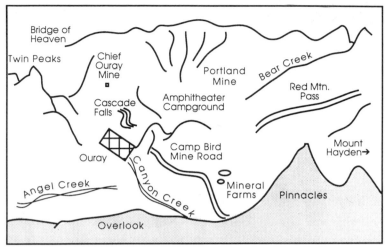

Bridge of Heaven

Twin Peaks

Chief Ouray Mine

Portland Mine

Bear Creek

Red Mtn. Pass

Cascade Falls

Amphitheater Campground

Ouray

Canyon Creek

Camp Bird Mine Road

Mineral Farms

Mount Hayden→

Pinnacles

Angel Creek

Overlook

ALPINE MINE OVERLOOK - View Looking East

of gentle switchbacks which meander through brush, aspen and alpine meadow. Almost immediately, great views open up across the valley. Look for the remains of the old Cutler Mine across the valley. After about 15 minutes, at a switchback the trail appears to go straight, also left. Take the left fork. Further up you can see some of the best views possible of Hayden Mountain which dominate the skyline across Canyon Creek to the east. The peaks themselves get higher as you look to the right and exceed 13,000 feet on the far right horizon.

After 45 minutes or so the Weehawken Creek opens up to the left with its towering cliffs on the far side. The trail continues up through a fine open aspen forest and reaches a little pass where there is a post. This point is reached after about one hour and is a good resting place. (Continuing on up in the valley is the Weehawken Creek Trail.)

Our trail bears right at this point up through more aspen, piñon pine, and spruce. After another 35 minutes or so the trail climbs up a grassy knoll and five minutes later comes to an overlook position. If you glance across the valley in front of you in the direction of Ouray (which is not visible from here) you can see a large rock feature on the skyline. This is our objective.

From the overlook, the trail goes sharp left past a pointed volcanic rock and curves its way in a concave arc around to the North. This portion of the trail is fairly level but follows a narrow ledge at times that can be slippery. Having traversed this short

Becky at the old Alpine Mine

stretch safely, the trail now climbs again to reach the site of the old Alpine Mine in another fifteen minutes.

From the mine the trail goes right but as a short detour it is interesting to look for the old cabin site located about 70 feet up on the left some 40 yards up the trail from the mine.

After another five minutes of walking, a second overlook position is reached where you can get good views down to the left. This is our high elevation point but it is another 300 yards or so to the final destination.

From the overlook, continue on the trail now going southeast. This follows the crest of a ridge and for some the trail may appear to be nonexistent but persevere - it is actually there and continues all the way to the final overlook at 10,944 feet. Here you will see two huge pinnacles to the right and, in the event it is windy and exposed (which it usually is) there is a good shelter in the small trees just to the left. Be careful, however, of the sheer drop off in front.

From this wonderful vantage point you can clearly see Twin Peaks to the left at the same elevation, Chief Ouray Mine in the Amphitheater with Bridge of Heaven above it on the skyline, Bear Creek going up at three o'clock with the Million Dollar Highway to Red Mountain Pass below it and, to the right, the magnificent panorama of the Hayden peaks. The two little lakes below are part of Mineral Farms Subdivision. This view is undoubtedly one of the best and I guarantee no one will feel unrewarded.

5. WEEHAWKEN/WEEHAWKEN CREEK

Elevation:	Start 8700 feet
	End of Trail 10,400 feet
Time:	Ouray to start point- 8 minutes (by car)
	Start to junction of Weehawken/Alpine Mine trails - 1 hour
	Junction to end of Weehawken Trail- 1.25 hours
	Return- 1.25 hours
	Total round trip- allow 4.5 hours
Map:	USGS Topographical Ironton
Difficulty:	Moderate

GENERAL DESCRIPTION

This trail shares the same initial one hour climb to an obvious junction point where the trail splits, with the right fork proceeding to Alpine Mine Overlook and main trail, (keeping left), following the Weehawken Creek. Generally speaking it is a gentle trail with much of it in woods. The first part is particularly beautiful as it ascends through spruce, aspen and open meadows with beautiful views back across the valley to Hayden Mountain.

The total round trip is 6 miles with no water on the trail for the first hour.

THE TRAIL

Start Point: 2.7 miles up the Camp Bird Mine Road on the right. Go south from Ouray on Highway 550 and turn right after the first switchback on County Road 361 which goes to Camp Bird and Yankee Boy Basin. After 2 miles, cross a bridge and proceed another .7 mile. Look for small opening on the right with Weehawken Trail sign. There is parking space here for about 4 vehicles and more space on the opposite side of the road.

Proceed up this very well maintained trail through a series

*Rugged skyline below Whitehouse Mountain from
10,400 feet near the top of Weehawken Creek*

of gentle switchbacks which meander through brush, aspen and alpine meadow. Almost immediately, great views open up across the valley where you can look for the remains of the old Cutler Mine. Further up you can see some of the best views possible of the Mt. Hayden peaks which dominate the skyline across Canyon Creek to the east.

After 45 minutes or so the Weehawken Creek opens up to the left with its towering cliffs on the far side. The trail continues up through a fine open aspen forest and reaches a little pass where there is a post which should indicate straight (west) for Weekhawken Creek and right (north) for Alpine Mine. From here the trail keeps left and proceeds through a steep alpine meadow above the creek. Looking up the valley you can see the main features of Whitehouse Mountain, while to the left, across the creek a massive wall rising to 11,500 feet runs all the way up to the end of the valley.

To the right and above of the trail are impressive pinnacles of volcanic origin.

After about 15 minutes, cross a well-defined stream and look for the trail about 30 yards to the right on the other side.

Cross two more smaller streams and, after another 20 minutes, climb steeply up a set of switchbacks for a 200 foot elevation gain. Just before this set of switchbacks, and just after another stream crossing, there may be a newly erected sign pointing down left to the Weehawken Mine. This little detour trail is not maintained and, hardly merits the extra ten minutes down to the mine, which consists mainly of an old collapsed building. The path down is a straight shot diagonally, you will see tailings on the right and an ore cart to the left in the trees. From there, go left horizontally about 200 yards to the building. Excluding this detour and after a few minutes of walking on the higher ground above the switchbacks, through a spruce forest, cross a small ravine looking for the trail slightly downstream on the other side.

Shortly afterwards the trail converges with the creek at a small open grassy meadow with another stream coming in from the right. Just before this it is interesting to look down at the main creek and see a large smooth log spanning the creek with a boulder lodged under it, exactly in the middle. One side of this log is wedged perfectly in a type of crevice in a large rock, and the other side is buried in the far bank. No modern engineer could have designed a more perfect or structurally strong bridge!

The trail continues clearly upstream (on the right of the creek) for another 600 yards, crossing two more streams coming in from the right and then comes to a rocky, gravelly open area with a dense area of spruce ahead. This is the end of the trail from where it is possible to see some really rugged rock formations ahead with Weehawken Creek itself turning left (southwest) up towards Potosi Peak.

This end point is sufficient to most hikers but, for the adventurous it is possible to proceed, although the country is inhospitable. Follow the dry stream bed on the right up towards the base of the rock spires going northward and then bear left, cross another branch of the creek and keep on the high ground to the right. As the main creek bears west, you can see the alpine meadow stretching up to the 11,000 foot contour line and one can head towards this and explore further following the creek up in a southwesterly direction, then up into the meadow and cliffs to the north.

Although interesting and extremely different terrain, this area is bear and mountain lion country and caution is advised.

6. CORBETT CREEK

Elevation:	Start point - 7,600 feet
	Top (Corbett Creek) - 9,100 feet
	Top Dallas Trail - 9,600 feet
	Top Moonshine Park - 9,700 feet
	Elevation gain - 1500 to 2100 feet
Time:	Start point to top of Corbett Creek Trail - 2.25 hours
	Top of Corbett Creek across to Dallas Trail - 45 minutes
	Dallas Trail junction to Moonshine Park - 45 minutes
	Dallas Trail junction to bottom - 1.25 hours
	Moonshine Park to bottom - 1.75 hours
	Top of Corbett Creek to bottom - 1.5 hours
	Allow 4 hours for the Corbett Creek hike
	Allow 5 hours for the Corbett Creek/Dallas Trail Loop
	Allow 6 hours for the Corbett Creek/Dallas /Moonshine Park hike (trail itself)
Map:	USGS Topographical Ouray
Difficulty:	Moderate

GENERAL DESCRIPTION

This is a very pleasant trail which keeps under 10,000 feet and therefore is not taxing as far as elevation is concerned. It is not frequented as much as many other trails and has its own blend of beauty, grandeur, and character. The Corbett Creek Trail follows the creek up for a couple of miles and then joins a tributary of the main creek for the top point. However, if time and energy permit, a loop can be made on a good trail by traversing north for a mile and then connecting with the lower

23

portion of the Dallas Trail which returns to the same start point. Another excursion can be made by going on up to a beautiful open meadow with stunning views called Moonshine Park and then returning on the Dallas Trail.

None of the trail is particularly strenuous and it is all below tree line.Water is scarce and the trail is also used by horses. Total distance for the Corbett Creek return trip is 5 miles. With the Dallas Loop it is 6 miles, and with the detour to Moonshine Park it is 8.5 miles.

THE TRAIL

Drive north out of Ouray for 2.3 miles until you come to a new concrete bridge across the Uncompahgre River on the left. Drive over the bridge and take the first sharp right which parallels the river for 100 yards and then, after .4 miles, come to a small stream with a rocky area just past it. Park on the right or left of the road and look for a small sign on the cliff side saying "Dallas Trailhead." This is the trail. After 50 yards another sign says "Dallas Trail." Continue up steep switchbacks for a few minutes and then note that the trail actually crosses an old road and continues on up through pine and scrub oak. After about 20 minutes of walking the trail comes out into an opening with fine views across the valley and up Dexter Creek. The trail proceeds past a small cairn and winds back south on the level for 300 yards until it reaches the cliffs above Corbett Creek which can be seen a hundred feet below on the left. In another few minutes the trail comes to an obvious junction, turn right here (west).There will be a sign for Corbett Creek and Dallas Trail. Bear left following the Corbett Creek sign and climb steeply for 15 minutes until you come to what looks like a pleasant campsite on the right. The trail bears left here on up the hill.

After about one hour (from the start) of walking and following the trail up the line of Corbett Creek, take the steep switchback to the right. At the next switchback go left, not straight, and wind up a beautiful stretch of trail parallel to the creek with superb views up the valley to Corbett Ridge ahead. Note the waterfall up to the left as you walk through very fine specimens of mature oak and piñon. After 15 minutes a flat area

Corbett Creek Valley (photographed in winter) —
trail goes up main valley and branches right

is reached with very large boulders and evidence of mining activity, an old wood cabin and stone-built structures. This is good shady place for a rest! From here the trail continues past a fallen tree and then immediately goes left, before the pile of rocks, into the oak. It is a little difficult to see but becomes an obvious trail again in about 20 yards before it meanders through and over another rocky area and then climbs again into a small stand of aspen. After about a 300 ft. elevation gain , the trail comes to a pleasant rock scree overlook - probably the remains of an old mine. From here you can look back across the valley at the same elevation to the sites of the old American Nettie and Jonathan Mines. The scenic ridge above Ouray is the Amphitheater topping out at 12,338 feet. Continuing on up, the trail passes through a really beautiful flower-filled glade before re-entering some very large spruce trees. Then follows a most idyllic setting of aspen forest lined with ferns, delphiniums and other alpine wildflowers (seen best in early summer). As you reach the top of the aspen grove, the trail comes to a definite T-junction. For the end of the Corbett Creek Trail (and a good resting place or lunch break) go left and continue for about 5 minutes through the aspen and spruce to a horse camp (for hunters) and down to a pleasant little creek. This is actually the west fork of Corbett Creek.

From here the decision should be made either to return on the same route or go back to the T-junction and instead of turning right to go back down, carry on straight for about a mile through the trees to connect with the main Dallas Trail at another creek due north of the T. If you choose to take the connecting trail to the Dallas Trail it climbs gently over the 9600 foot contour and takes about 40 to 50 minutes. Then, at the Dallas Creek junction, another choice is possible. Option 1: go straight on to come down through spruce and aspen for about 2 miles to the original junction point of the Corbett Creek/ Dallas Trail. If you do this the trail descends sharply at first and then flattens out at a point where the trail would be mistaken for going straight ahead north through a meadow. DO NOT go straight but turn sharp right and continue downhill past an old mine with a cabin which has had a large tree fall right on top of it. Option 2: turn left across the creek and continue on up the Dallas Trail for about 45 minutes to Moonshine Park. For those who decide to do this, the reward is worth it. It is an outstandingly beautiful sloping meadow surrounded by aspen with exceptional views across to the Cimarron Mountains and up towards Ouray. It is also a great place to see elk and bighorn sheep. (The Dallas Trail itself makes a long sweep round the east of the San Juan Sneffels Range and eventually comes out near Telluride on the north side. Much of the trail goes through private land and at times it is intermittent and hard to find. At Moonshine Park look for a post and then for a second post about 100 yards up to the right. From the second post, the trail heads up the meadow to the aspen trees at top left and then enters private property through a gate.

The descent from Moonshine Park to the trailhead takes just under two hours and consists of returning to the creek and then turning left to continue down the Dallas Trail until you come to the original junction of the Dallas and Corbett Trails. Bear left and return to the start point on the main trail.

7. OAK CREEK

Elevation:	Start 8200 feet
	Oak Creek crossing 9400 feet
	End of trail 10,700 feet
Time:	Ouray to start point 5 minutes (by car)
	Start to Oak Creek crossing 1.25 hours
	Oak Creek crossing to top 1.25 hours
	Return 1.5 hours
	Total round trip - allow - 4 to 5 hours
Map:	USGS Topographical Ouray
Difficulty:	Moderate

GENERAL DESCRIPTION

This trail is mainly shaded and unexposed. There are magnificent views of Oak Creek and waterfalls and it is possible to make the hike shorter by just going to the creek crossing if you don't want to continue up to the end of the trail. Up to the creek crossing the trail is very well maintained. After that it is not. This is a trail that is not frequented often and is therefore delightful because of it's untrampled quality. It is just under 1 mile to the creek and about 2.25 miles to the trail end overlook.

THE TRAIL

Start Point: Off of Oak Street
* SEE MAP (next page)

There is room for several vehicles to park at the trail head. Start by heading up the trail for 40 yards and keep straight on. Do not go left. Climb up the switchbacks through scrub oak, juniper and ponderosa pine. After about 20 minutes there are great views up Canyon Creek towards Camp Bird Mine. The mountain at the head of the valley is US Mountain (13,036 ft.) and the rocky outcrop up on the right is the Alpine Mine overlook (offshoot of Weehawken Trail).

In another 10 minutes the trail enters a spruce forest from

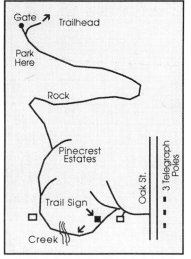 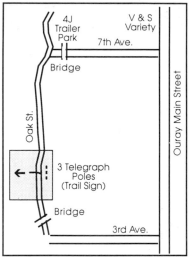

DETAIL OF TRAIL MAP (at right)   **OAK CREEK / TWIN PEAKS TRAIL**

where it is possible to see Twin Peaks up to the right. Just ahead, about 45 minutes from the start, the trail splits at a clearly marked sign. To the right is the Twin Peaks Trail and to the left is the Oak Creek Trail. Stay left even though you can hear the roar of Oak Creek to the right.

After a few minutes there is a great view across Canyon Creek of the grassy triangular top of Mount Hayden (12,687 feet). Ten minutes later the trail goes through a glade of aspen and then heads up back towards the creek. This next stretch is fairly well on the flat and you can hear the roar of Oak Creek 500 feet below to the right as it rises rapidly to meet the trail a little further on. As you near the crossing point, look for the cascading waterfalls below.

At Oak Creek itself there is a good place to rest and enjoy the energy and therapeutic effects of the tumbling creek.

Now cross the creek looking for the best place which may vary according to conditions. The trail picks up on the far side going to the right and then switchbacks on and up following the path of the creek which is now on your left. After .25 mile look for superb views of waterfalls and just ahead notice the two horizontal mine shafts right on the trail to the right. Carry

Oak Creek Trail, near top, looking up towards Whitehouse Mountain

on up through dense spruce for another 15 minutes to an open meadow, approximately 45 minutes after crossing the creek. On the climb up to the meadow it is worth looking back down to see if you can catch a glimpse of Ouray following the path of Oak Creek itself. From the meadow the trail is poorly marked and maintained. Look for a 6 foot high stake in the ground and follow a trail through thick foliage and wildflowers to another stake about 200 yards ahead and slightly to the right. From here, head up the slope to the right through aspen via a series of switchbacks. Keep the rock pinnacles to your right and the trail will eventually come back towards them as it actually goes just above them. As you climb this slope it is still possible to see old trail blaze markers but early in the season fallen trees may be encountered. At the "top" the trail continues east to the base of another pinnacle rock. This is the end of the trail and is sometimes marked by a small pile of stones on the trail. From here there are great views looking ahead up Oak Creek to a grassy saddle above which the towering mantle of Whitehouse Mountain (13,492 feet) dominates the skyline. To the east it is possible to see a fine perspective of the Amphitheater with Engineer Mountain and Mount Hayden to the southeast. You can also get a glimpse of the Million Dollar Highway below and the start of the Engineer Pass Road as it bears up off of Highway 550.

Contrary to what some people have said, there is no real trail that links the top of this one with Twin Peaks and I would not recommend that the idea of a loop be pursued as the terrain here is extremely dense and rugged. There is, however, a less discernible trail which heads back west from the pile of stones up into the spruce trees and then turns north to go over a divide before heading back down to Silvershield Mine and Highway 550 about 1.5 miles north of Ouray. This particular trail is entirely in trees with little or no views and often is virtually impossible to accurately determine where the trail is. I therefore, do not recommend it unless plenty of extra time is allowed and knowledge of what to do if lost is readily available.

8. BALDY

Elevation:	Start - 8700 feet
	Top - 10,603 feet
Time:	From Ouray to trailhead by vehicle - 20 minutes
	From trailhead to top - 2 to 2.5 hours
	From top to bottom - 1.25 hours
	Allow 4 to 5 hours for round trip
Map:	USGS Topographical Ouray and Wetterhorn
Difficulty:	Moderate

GENERAL DESCRIPTION

Baldy is a relatively easy trail which is a favorite of mine. Although not rising much above 10,000 feet it offers some of the best views and scenery of any trail and is particularly suitable to hike at the beginning or end of the hiking season. However, any time between Memorial Day and mid-October will offer different and wonderful new perspectives of the Sneffels and Cimarron Ranges.

The round trip for the trail to the top of Baldy itself is about 5 miles but another excellent vantage turn around point reduces this to 4 miles if you don't want to leave the main trail to free-walk up the final slopes to the summit.

THE TRAIL

Drive north towards Ridgway for 2.2 miles and look for the Dexter Creek Road going off the main Highway 550 to the right. This is County Road 14. Proceed past the Panoramic Heights Subdivision on the left and on past Lake Lenore to the junction of County Road 14 and 14A. Bear left across a bridge (over Dexter Creek) on road 14A. After a mile pass a sign saying Uncompahgre National Forest and go on past some old wooden mining equipment. At the crest of the hill keep left on the better road and descend keeping on the better road despite numerous

Sneffels Range in late September from near the top of Baldy Trail

smaller offshoots. At the bottom of the decline there is a field to the right. Keep left and descend down a short steep stretch to a creek (Cutler Creek). Cross this creek and continue past the Cutler Creek Trailhead sign to an aspen tree area and meadow. Here the road gets a little rough, but if possible, continue on for another quarter of a mile to another small creek. Cross and park immediately on the far side where the jeep road turns a sharp left. Just opposite this, on the right hand side is the Baldy Trailhead. The total distance from the Dexter Creek turn-off to this trailhead is 3.3 miles.

The trail follows the left side of the stream for 100 yards and then splits. Go left, away from the stream (which leads up to Stormy Gulch), and start to climb gently up the slope in front of you through beautiful stands of mature scrub oak interspersed with juniper and occasional aspen. The trail continues for about an hour up through this fine country past two or three beautiful little meadows (one with an old round horse or cattle trough by a spring), up past an impressive group of rock cliffs and eventually into a more open area before topping out at a ridge at 9700 feet. The views get better and better with increased elevation and one can see new panoramas of the Sneffels Range, Corbett Creek and the valleys above Ouray.

At the ridge line, which has pine and spruce trees on it, go right (east) and continue on this ridge as it gains elevation in and out of the trees and past a beautiful aspen stand on the left. Here, on a fine day it is possible to see both the La Sal Mountains and the Henries in Utah way over behind the Uncompahgre Plateau to the west. There are also tantalizing views of the tops of peaks like Wetterhorn and Uncompahgre Peak to the east.

Further on, another group of mountains begin to appear to the north. These are the Cimarrons with Chimney Peak and Courthouse Rock being most dominant.

About 50 minutes or so from the ridge at 9700 feet after coming up through another superb meadow of aspens another ridge is reached at an elevation of 10,400 feet. On the right one can experience the magnificent vista of the Cimarrons rising above and beyond Cow Creek down below.

This point, just before the trail goes back into the spruce trees and heads sharp right, is a good place to rest or end the hike before returning. Baldy Peak itself can be clearly seen about half a mile to the left (due west). To get to the top takes another 20 minutes and the best route is to follow the line of trees going to the left, keeping this side of them in the open and just head on up to the wooden cross and USGS markers at the top (10,603 feet). If you do this you will get even more spectacular views of the entire Sneffels Range and up the Uncompahgre Valley towards Delta and beyond, as well as the Cimarrons from Storm King right round to the backside of the Amphitheater.

For those who want to continue walking, it is possible to stay on the trail, turn right at the trees ahead which is at about 10,500 feet and continue on for several miles following the tree covered ridge line above 10,000 feet to eventually link up with the top of Dexter Creek Trail, but some of this trail is not well marked and it would not be advisable to try to do the whole thing in one day especially without USGS Topographical maps of Ouray and Wetterhorn.

9. BEAR CREEK

TO GRIZZLY BEAR MINE AND/OR YELLOW JACKET MINE

Elevation:	Start - 8400 feet. Grizzly Bear 10,050 feet. Yellow Jacket 11,100 feet.
Time:	Ouray to start point (by car) 10 minutes Start to Grizzly Bear 1.5 hours Grizzly Bear to Yellow Jacket 1 hour 20 minutes Return Yellow Jacket to Grizzly Bear 1 hour Return Grizzly Bear to start point 50 minutes Total round trip to Grizzly Bear allow 3.5 hours (trail itself) Total round trip to Yellow Jacket allow 6 hours (trail itself)
Map:	USGS Topo. Ouray, Ironton, Handies Peak
Difficulty:	Moderate

GENERAL DESCRIPTION

This trail is one of the most diverse trails in the state. It is steep in parts and has many areas of exposure with drop off of 200 feet or more. Views change continuously. The hike to grizzly Bear Mine is 2.5 miles. Yellow Jacket is another 1.7 miles further and is a less steep climb. Not recommended for young children. Lots of old mine equipment and buildings. No water for first 1.25 hours.

THE TRAIL: (FOREST SERVICE TRAIL NUMBER 241)

Start Point: Go south on Highway 550 (Million Dollar Highway) for 2 miles until you reach a small tunnel. Immediately after going through the tunnel, park on the left hand side of the road. The trail starts opposite on the right hand side of the road and immediately climbs back over the roof of the tunnel.

From the sign-in box the trail climbs steeply up for about a thousand feet traversing old slate slides. Take time to admire some wonderful old juniper and pine trees and see if you can remember to count the switchbacks so that they don't total an unlucky number! Also, take in great views up to Red Mountain Pass on the Million Dollar Highway with majestic Mt. Abrams to the left.

After about an hour the trail follows Bear Creek and is literally carved out of the rock cliff. Here, ponderosa and spruce trees thrive as do roses and wild raspberries. This part of the trail is the most dangerous and all hikers need to concentrate on safety. Across the creek it is possible to see numerous mine holes cut horizontally into the cliff.

A few minutes later, after walking through a small aspen stand, the trail crosses a narrow wooden bridge. From there you can see the old telephone and power lines crossing the canyon to the other side. Here there are extreme drop off and extra care is required.

In another five minutes or so a small stream is crossed and the trail starts to climb again through aspen with beautiful vegetation and flowers. Very soon you see a shed up on the hill to the left and just ahead of this is a mass of heavy mining equipment used by the Grizzly Bear Mine. Go another 200 yards and see the remains of a wooden building down on the right. There is a bench outside and this makes an excellent place for a rest stop.

At this point the decision should be made either to continue to Yellow Jacket Mine or return.

To continue to Yellow Jacket, follow the trail east keeping the creek on the right. Look for a mine shaft hole on your left. Shortly you will probably be able to see one or more snowfields covering the creek. These are the results of avalanche slides from the other side of the creek and in some years they never fully melt.

The trail continues gently until it reaches the level of the creek and then, at a post in the ground, it climbs sharply up to the left with a few steep switchbacks, and comes down again to the creek about 400 yards ahead. Do not try to take the short-cut

Yellow Jacket Mine on the Bear Creek Trail

here as the area is seriously eroded. A little farther on the trail re-enters a spruce forest. Note the old cabin on the right. Then, about 25 minutes after leaving Grizzly Bear you come to a marker post at a stream coming in from the left. Look for the marker post on the other side of the stream to find the trail beyond but go a little to the left to find the best place to cross the stream. Five minutes later enter a beautiful lush meadow with stunning views back towards the north side of the amphitheater, an attractive peak up to the left (12,000 feet), and an unnamed peak straight ahead of 13,132 feet.

From here the trail climbs again up switchbacks for 300 yards. It is worth taking time to look across the ravine to a mine hole on the other side and watch for a beautiful but fairly obscure waterfall across the creek.

Cross another smaller stream and continue on up through meadows of aspen and spruce for another 20 minutes before arriving at the Yellow Jacket Mine site. On the left is a huge pile of debris and remains of mining equipment and machinery and on the right is a building in good shape with a classic outhouse to the right.

This site is pristine in its beauty and a photographer's

dream. It is right at the confluence of Bear Creek and another creek coming down from the north.

Although this is the end of the hike, it is possible to continue east, crossing the fast moving creek and following Bear Creek for about .25 mile with buildings on the right until you reach a marker post which indicates that Engineer Pass can be reached after 3 miles and Horsethief Trail (to the left) is 2 miles. It is this Horsethief Trail which, after traversing American Flats at about 12,000 feet in a northwesterly direction, eventually meets the to Bridge of Heaven and returns westward to Dexter Creek. However, this is considered a full two day overnight hike and definitely not recommended for those without considerable experience.

10. DEXTER CREEK

Elevation:	Start - 8600 feet
	Top - 11,404 feet
Time:	From Ouray to trailhead by vehicle - 12 minutes
	From trailhead to top - 3.5 to 4 hours
	From top to bottom - 2 hours
	Total round trip - allow 6 to 7 hours (trail itself)
Map:	USGS Topographical Ouray and Wetterhorn
Difficulty:	Moderate

GENERAL DESCRIPTION

This is a most pleasant trail which essentially winds up Dexter Creek and the north fork of Dexter Creek for about four miles before climbing steeply to a divide which overlooks Cow Creek and the Cimarron Range to the west.

There is a wonderful variety of wildflowers and vegetation on this trail and plenty of water. It starts gently and gets more difficult towards the top.

Most of the trail is shaded and there are lots of old buildings and mine machinery to explore in the first mile.

The trail is open to horses as well as hikers. The round trip to the top point of 11,404 feet is 10 miles from the start.

THE TRAIL

The drive from Ouray to the trailhead is on a good road. From Ouray, drive north for 2.2 miles and turn right on County Road 14 marked Dexter Creek. Wind up this road keeping the spectacular little Lake Lenore on your right and come to a junction at a bridge. Stay right on County Road 14 and a little further on stay left on the road that has a sign for Uncompahgre National Forest. Continue up the side of Dexter Creek and, after a total of 4.6 miles from Ouray, look for a large mine tailing pile on the left. Park here, on either side of the road.

Our trailhead is 20 yards further on across from a stand of aspen trees. It should be clearly marked "Dexter Creek Trailhead." Do not take the other trail which you can see heading up the mountain from the lower end of the mine tailings.

The trail starts out following Dexter Creek and then turns left through spruce, cottonwood, alder, and aspen trees for 300 yards to cross a dry creek coming in from the left at a cairn (pile of rocks). There should be a trail sign here (number 205) with smaller markers on the trees going up the trail on the other side. It climbs for about 200 feet and then follows Dexter Creek again going east on level ground through scrub oak. Note the old brick encased boiler on the right.

Proceed on through a pleasant aspen stand and back into spruce. Look for three or four mine buildings, down to the right. This is the old Almadi Mine Complex.

A little further on there is a well preserved corrugated iron building up to the left with a log cabin close by and some heavy mining machinery on the right.

From here the trail maintains the same elevation and, after just over half and hour from the start point, crosses a dry creek. Then cross a second dry creek and follow Dexter Creek up and around a curve to a point where the trail takes an obvious left turn up and away from the creek. You might notice a lesser trail going off to the right following the creek but stay on the one going uphill.

After a stiff climb the trail reaches a point where it opens up considerably and it is possible to get good views up the valley. (The trail goes up the valley and then to the left).

The trail now descends a little to cross a double dry creek. Look for the trail blaze sign on a tree, a little upstream on the other side and wind up the farthest of the two creeks (actually between them) for about 100 yards to a cairn.

Now cross the farthest creek and rejoin the main trail switchbacking up through spruce trees to another cairn where the trail leaves the creek and starts to climb steeply for about 20

Old mning machinery at Dexter Creek Trail

minutes before reaching the start of a ridge. Here there is a sign indicating that you are now entering the Big Blue Wilderness Area. Elevation here is 9800 feet and time taken to this point is approximately 1.5 hours.

Proceed up the ridge for 10 minutes to a beautiful grassy aspen slope then on back into the spruce. Climb up until you see a man-made fence or corral on the left and go on up to what appears to be the head of the valley which now turns left and continues up another smaller narrow valley. The mountainous walls up on the right are part of the ridge line on which Bridge of Heaven sits majestically overlooking the Amphitheater on the far side.

The small creek we are now following is not actually Dexter Creek and takes us northwest up through a beautiful area of dense lush vegetation and flowers. The trail crosses the stream two or three times and climbs up past an obvious avalanche chute with lots of downed trees and snow still visible over the stream. Above this is a large rock slide on the right. Then comes an open area before the trail turns sharp left to climb up steeply towards an interesting rock spire with a camp site close by.

From here the trail bears right up the grassy slope and

steeply climbs diagonally back into the trees. Here the trail deteriorates and has lots of fallen trees. However if you look for the numerous trail blaze signs, it is not too difficult to keep on the trail, despite the obstacles. About here, an interesting peak appears up to the right. It has no name but is just over a thousand feet higher at 12,444 feet. Continue up through dense spruce until you see what looks like a bare hilltop to the right with a large old fallen log lying horizontally across it. From here, bear right up a little ridge, from where fine views of the Cimarrons, Cow Creek, Cutler Creek and Baldy Peak are available, and proceed on back into the spruce for another ten minutes. Suddenly the trail becomes much better as it tops out on the high point and a few minutes later the end of the trail is reached at a sign which says Dexter Creek 2, Bachelor Mine 5.

Most hikers will probably wish to return from here but it is possible to carry on (turning left at the sign) and follow the ridge round to the West for about another 6 miles to the Cutler Creek jeep road.

11. BLUE LAKES

Elevation:	Start 9400 feet Lower Lake 11,000 feet Upper Lakes 11,700 feet
Time::	Ouray to start point - 45 minutes (by car) Start to Lower Lake - 2 hours Lower Lake to Upper Lakes - 45 minutes Return from Lower Lake to trailhead - 1.25 hours Total round-trip - allow 5-7 hours (trail itself)
Map:	USGS Topographical Mt. Sneffels
Difficulty:	Moderate-Difficult

GENERAL DESCRIPTION

This trail is a beautiful hike leading up to the glacial lakes at the foot of Mt. Sneffels on the Northwest side.

The drive to the trailhead takes about 45 minutes, but is particularly scenic.

The trail is not difficult to the Lower Blue Lake but is steep from there to the Upper Lakes, where it breaks out above timber line into tundra. Although fishing is possible in all the lakes I have not heard of great success.

Vegetation and scenery are varied and the views in places are breathtaking, especially on the escarpment leading up to the Upper Lakes.

THE TRAIL (FOREST SERVICE TRAIL #201)

Drive north to Ridgway on Highway 550. Turn left at Ridgway on Highway 62 and drive West for 4.8 miles where there is a new road-bridge. Turn left here onto the East Dallas Creek National Forest access road. From here it is 9 miles on a good gravel road to the Blue Lakes Trailhead parking area. Keep left at the Uncompahgre National Forest access road sign; a little further on bear right—do not go left on County Road 7A, but keep on the Uncompahgre National Forest access road.

Further on the road opens out with a magnificent valley down to the right at the end of which are excellent camping facilities. Views of Mt. Sneffels from here are superb.

Proceed past this spot keeping on the "main" road, crossing the East Dallas Creek to the small parking area at the end.

The trail starts at the metal gate. Proceed towards the mountain for 100 yards and look for the Blue Lakes Trailhead on the right.

Lower Blue Lake from the trail leading up to two upper lakes

The trail starts up to the right (west) of East Dallas Creek, which it follows for sometime before continuing up through beautiful meadows and wild flowers with a combination of switchbacks and level trail through spruce forest. After about 50 minutes the Mt. Sneffels wilderness area is reached and 10 minutes further on, the trail crosses a pleasant creek coming in from the right. On the other side it enters a small meadow before returning to a spruce forest and more switchbacks. After another 20 minutes, an open area offers fine views of the peaks surrounding the Lower Blue Lake Basin ahead with Mt. Sneffels rising up to the east (left side) and east Dallas Creek below. In the distance looking back downstream, the Uncompahgre Valley can be seen. The body of water is the Ridgway Reservoir and above it, on the northern horizon, is the West Elk Mountain Range near Paonia.

After crossing the open area (which is an avalanche path in the winter) the trail continues through spruce trees for another

43

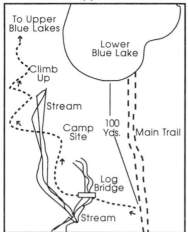

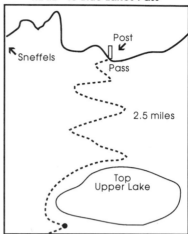

20 minutes before reaching the northern end of the Lower Blue Lake. Many good resting places can be found here or by going to the right up the western side of the lake.

For many this point is the end of the trail, but for the more ambitious and relatively fit, it is worth continuing on up to two lakes situated about 600 to 700 feet higher and up to the left towards Mt. Sneffels. To do this go back and to the right a little and cross a log bridge over one fork of the East Dallas Creek followed by another fork (this time without a bridge) and head up directly towards the steep western shoulder of Sneffels. From here the trail traverses up the rocky cliff feature for about 30 minutes and then opens out onto grassy tundra. After another 10 minutes the first Upper Lake is reached which is down to the left of the trail. There are superb views down to the Lower Blue Lake from the trail leading up the ridge. In another few minutes the trail comes to the second Upper Lake. This should be considered the end of this trail although you will see that it actually goes around the left side of the lake and switchbacks steeply up the wall in front to reach Blue Lake Pass at 12,960 feet.

[From the pass one can descend to Yankee Boy Basin or climb up the wide couloir on the other side from which the main Yankee Boy Basin route to the Sneffels summit is reached. However, either of these options makes an extremely long day unless two vehicles are pre-positioned accordingly].

12. UPPER CASCADE FALLS

CHIEF OURAY MINE

Elevation:	Start - 8500 feet (from Amphitheater Campground)
	Top - 10,000 feet
Time:	From Ouray to trailhead by vehicle - 10 minutes
	From trailhead to top - 1.5 to 2 hours
	From top to bottom - 1 hour
	Allow 3.5 to 4.5 hours for round trip
Map:	USGS Topographical Ouray
Difficulty:	Moderate-Difficult

GENERAL DESCRIPTION

This is a shorter trail which literally starts a few minutes from downtown Ouray. The elevation gain of 1500 feet allows good exercise and the trail is very well maintained. It provides magnificent views of a waterfall at the top and ends up at the Chief Ouray Mine bunkhouse and machinery buildings. From this second building, there is an outstanding view down to Ouray 2300 feet below, as well as straight line views up Canyon Creek to Camp Bird and the Uncompahgre gorge through which the Million Dollar Highway winds its way down from Red Mountain Pass.

It can be very hot on this trail in the Summer although the first half hour of the trail is particularly beautiful, sheltered, and picturesque. It is a good idea to look for the Chief Ouray Mine about two thirds the way up in the amphitheater over to the left, from the center of town, to gain a true perspective of where the trail destination is, before leaving.

The round trip for the trail itself is 4.25 miles.

THE TRAIL (FOREST SERVICE TRAIL NUMBER 213)

To reach the start point, drive south out of Ouray on

Highway 550 for 1.3 miles past the turn off for Box Canyon Falls and Yankee Boy Basin to the second switchback. Turn left at the sign which says Uncompahgre National Forest Campground - Amphitheater. Go up this road for 1 mile to the end where there is a turn-around point and small parking area.

The trailhead is clearly marked "Upper Cascade Falls" at the far end on the right. If the gate to the Amphitheater Campground is closed (before or after the season) you will either have to park and walk up the road to the Campground or access the trail by starting out on the Portland Mine Trail (page 14) and follow it up until you reach a junction with a sign which shows the Upper Cascade Falls Trail going off to the left.

Start by climbing a little and then on level ground through scrub oak on a grass-lined path for .25 mile before coming to a junction. Bear left here for Chief Ouray Mine and start climbing steeply for 200 feet before leveling out again and proceeding gently up through a beautiful section of spruce, ponderosa pine, juniper, and oak, interspersed with lovely shady meadows and green vegetation.

Note that it is not possible to see the Chief Ouray Mine at all until the very top.

After about 25 or 30 minutes you come to another junction where, again, the left fork should be taken. From here the trail follows the left (north) side of the Portland Creek from where it is possible to see activity in the working Portland Mine straight ahead and up to the right.

About 20 minutes later the trail takes a definite sharp left turn and starts to climb significantly. In fact there are eleven hefty switchbacks which take you up 700 feet fairly quickly. This is the hardest part of the trail, but rewarding because of that wonderful feeling of gaining elevation.

Depending on level of fitness and energy this section of the trail could take between 30 and 45 minutes or more. The rest of the trail is easy. At the top it levels out and winds around on a ledge for about 300 yards to a bend with a rock feature with a slit in it on the left side of the trail. On rounding this bend a great view opens up to the north, of the Uncompahgre Valley. The pile of rocks on the left offer a super platform for photos of

Canyon Creek where Camp Bird Mine can be seen clearly with United States Mountain (13,036 feet) at the head of the valley, with the striking Potosi Peak (13,786 feet) up on the right. Across the valley about 800 feet higher is the Twin Peaks feature which rises up from Oak Creek to its left.

Chief Ouray Mine

Also from this point can (at last!) be seen the Chief Ouray Mine buildings. Note that there are two separate buildings and both are on the far side of Cascade Creek. It is only from the second (farthest away) building that views to Ouray can be seen.

The walk to the creek takes under five minutes on an excellent trail and on reaching it the sound of two waterfalls - one above and one below the crossing, greets the hiker with unexpected exhilaration. This is, indeed, a refreshing and special place.

To get to the first building of Chief Ouray Mine, cross the creek and keep on the trail going west for about five minutes. There are drop offs here and care should be taken.

The building is the old bunk house and is still in good shape. If you walk through it the trail continues out the "back door" for another 300 yards around a bend in the cliffs to another smaller building perched on the top of a vertical rock cliff just above the old mine shaft. This building houses some heavy machinery and should be considered the end of the trail.

From here there are fantastic views down to the town of Ouray and surrounding peaks including Mount Hayden between Canyon Creek and the Red Mountain Pass Road.

13. BRIDGE OF HEAVEN

Elevation:	Start 9300 feet Top 12,300 feet
Time:	From Ouray to trailhead by car - 20-25 minutes From trailhead to top - 3 hours From top to bottom - 1.5 to 2 hours Allow 5.5 to 6 hours for round trip (trail only)
Map:	USGS Topographical Ouray
Difficulty:	Difficult

GENERAL DESCRIPTION

Although technically known as Horse Thief Trail (which goes from the start point of this trail all the way around the back side of the Amphitheater and back down Bear Creek Trail and which is considered a 2-day hike), this particular hike takes us up to a high point known as Bridge of Heaven.

Many consider this trail to be one of the finest in the area. Its starting point at 9300 feet gives it quite an advantage, and the very name "Bridge of Heaven" conjures up a wonderful dream of beauty and lofty vantage points with outstanding views and scenery. All of this is true. It is a moderately difficulty trail with no serious danger points, but hikers should note that there is absolutely no water the whole way up.

The round trip for the trail itself is a total of 8 miles.

THE TRAIL (FOREST SERVICE TRAIL NUMBER 215)

Start Point: The trailhead is 5.5 miles from Ouray going north on Highway 550. About 1.7 miles from the Ouray swimming pool, look for a sign on the right for Bachelor-Syracuse Mine and one on the left pointing to Dexter Creek. Turn right here on County Road 14 and proceed on up the gravel road following signs for the mine tour. Go past Lake Lenore and at a road junction with a bridge keep right on County Road 14. At

Looking west from the Bridge of Heaven up Canyon Creek as a storm gathers in the afternoon.

the next junction keep straight on. DO NOT turn right for the mine tour. Wind up the road following Dexter Creek for 1.3 miles. Here you will see some tailings and, just past them, another trailhead for the Dexter Creek trail. Continue on across the creek, and (if they are there!) follow signs for Horse Thief Trail. Directly across the creek bear left. Although a regular car may make it OK, 4-wheel drive vehicles are recommended beyond this point. After .25 mile go straight on (not left) and carry on up for another 1 mile until you see the mine tailings of the Wedge Mine on the left. You can either park here where there is plenty of room or drive on up a poor road for another 300 yards until you can see an open grassy meadow. The trailhead is clearly marked on the right and tells us the Bridge of Heaven is 4 miles, Difficulty Creek is 7 miles, American Flats is 9.5 miles, and Engineer Mountain is 11 miles.

Start by heading up into the spruce forest. After 15 or 20 minutes there are a couple of good overlooks to the right in an aspen grove but keep to the main trail going up left.

After another 15 minutes the trail opens out and follows switchbacks back up into the trees. At these switchbacks, look back west to see a fine view of Whitehouse Mountain across the valley and the Ridgway area to the north. After about 1 hour and 1.5 miles of hiking a grass knoll with a sign post is reached. From here a panorama of views opens up to reveal Ouray, Mt. Hayden, Red Mountain, Mt. Abrams, Camp Bird, and Imogene Pass.

Go left towards the Amphitheater. The trail actually continues to the left of a rocky outcrop back into trees before coming to a small open pass and then back again into trees, this time a beautiful aspen stand, above which is another grassy knoll and a good place to rest.

Proceed on up via a series of switchbacks through slopes of lupine and dwarf sunflower. At the next vantage point you can see North Pole Peak which is the little nipple at the far right of the ridge to the right of Whitehouse. This is the Northern-most peak in the San Juan Range. On a clear day you can also see the snow capped La Sal Mountain Range in Utah just to the northwest.

Now the trail goes up a ridge, in and out of trees. Look through the trees on the left for fine glimpses of Courthouse Rock and the Cimarron Range. This is about the 2 hour point.

After another 20 minutes, emerge out onto the base of a grassy hill towering above and to the left. Cross a small gully (which may have a snow field in it) and follow the trail traversing up to the top of this hill. The trail is now above the tree line. At nearly the top of the hill, the trail bears right and after another 100 yards arrives at a small open pass with 2 wood stakes. This is Bridge of Heaven!

Views from here include Montrose, Delta and Grand Mesa to the North, the Cimarrons, Uncompahgre Peak, and the Big Blue Wilderness Area to the east, the road up to Camp Bird Mine with the Sneffels Range to the west and Red Mountain Pass (Million Dollar Highway) with the valley of Ironton to the South. Far below on the other side of the pass is Dexter Creek.

You can also see the continuation of Horse Thief Trail descending back into the trees. This continues southeast for 3 miles to Difficulty Creek and eventually, after traversing 9 more miles of unmarked trail over American Flats, meets up with Bear Creek trail which leads down past Yellow Jacket and Grizzly Bear Mines to Highway 550 south of Ouray.

DO NOT, try this unless you are fully prepared to camp overnight; it is more than a one day hike!

14. TWIN PEAKS

Elevation:	Start 8200 feet
	Top 10,800 feet
Time:	From Ouray to trailhead by car - 5 minutes
	From trailhead to Oak Creek crossing- 45 minutes
	From Oak Creek to Twin Peaks summit- 2 hrs. 15 minutes
	From top to bottom- 2 hrs. 15 minutes
	Total round trip- allow 6 hours
Map:	USGS Topographical Ouray
Difficulty:	Difficult

GENERAL DESCRIPTION

This trail is a little deceptive. Although starting out virtually in Ouray itself and ascending some 2600 feet to the rock peaks clearly seen above on the west side, it is definitely one of the more demanding physically. After climbing steeply to cross Oak Creek the trail wanders around the front (Ouray) side of the Twin Peaks shoulder and then winds its way back up to an overlook point from the north. From here there is an extremely steep exposed climb up to the Twin Peaks feature, where it can be quite cold and windy. Nevertheless, it is a classic hike and one which offers a great deal of variety with a real summit and magnificent views of Ouray and surrounding mountains.

THE TRAIL

Start Point: Off of Oak Street

*See Map (next page)

There is room for several vehicles to park at the trailhead. Start by climbing up the trail for 40 yards and keep straight on. Do not go left. Climb up switchbacks through scrub oak, juniper and ponderosa pine. After about 20 minutes there are great views up Canyon Creek towards Camp Bird Mine. The

Distant view of Twin Peaks (taken from the Camp Bird Mine Road)

mountain at the head of the valley is US Mountain (13,036 ft.) and the rocky outcrop up on the right is the Alpine Mine overlook (Offshoot of Weehawken Trail).

In another 10 minutes the trail enters a spruce forest from where it is possible to see the Twin Peaks up to the right. Just ahead the trail splits at a clearly marked sign. The Oak Creek Trail goes to the left and our trail goes to the right. This point should be reached in about 45 minutes.

Follow the trail on the level, then gradually descend to cross the creek after about 8 minutes and proceed up the other side directly across the creek. The trail climbs a little and then continues on the level again with views of the Amphitheater to the east. After another 10 minutes the trail makes a switchback and then continues north on the level again with good views of Mount Abrams and Mount Hayden to the south and south-west. After another switchback the trail crosses a large clearing on the level and re-enters an aspen grove after about 300 yards. To the left is a big wall with a promontory on top. This is the sister peak, which is about 400 feet below the Twin Peaks summit. The trail then continues up and around to the east eventually coming to a sign post and turning back left into the

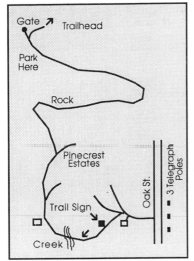

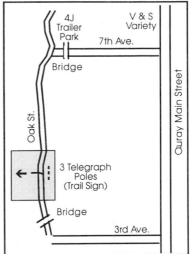

DETAIL OF TRAIL MAP (at right)   **OAK CREEK / TWIN PEAKS TRAIL**

aspen. This should be about 40 minutes past the creek. From here it is 1.5 miles to the top. Another 5 minutes ahead there is a meadow on the right which is a nice resting place before beginning the steep ascent which winds around to the north climbing past an old mine shaft and later an old log cabin. More switchbacks through dense spruce precede breaking out onto the open ridge with Sister Peak on the left and Twin Peaks farther up on the right. Turn right up the ridge following the steep trail about .25 mile all the way to the summit. Allow about 3 hours for the total climb to the top. In places the trail is steep and hiking boots are recommended. Don't forget the possibilities of changeable weather on this hike and be prepared for considerable exposure to wind and cold on the top ridge.

Having reached the top there are wonderful 360 degree views with Mt. Hayden to the south, Whitehouse to the west, the Amphitheater and Bridge of Heaven to the east, and Courthouse and the Coxcomb to the northwest.

15. BLAINE BASIN

Elevation:	Start point - 9400 feet
	Top (Basin) - 11,100 feet
	Top (Excursion) - 12,200 to 12,600 feet
Time:	Ouray to start point - 45 minutes (by vehicle)
	Start Point to top (Basin) - 2.25 hours
	Excursion - 1 hour plus
	Top to bottom - 1.5 to 2 hours
	Round trip (trail only) - allow 4.5 to 6 hours
Map:	USGS Topographical Mt. Sneffels
Difficulty:	Difficult

GENERAL DESCRIPTION

This hike is quite different to most in that it starts out easily on a disused dirt road and almost imperceptibly climbs gently over about three miles to suddenly reveal a most unusual landscape of classical glacial moraines at the foot of the north face of Sneffels. The trail is not well known and therefore not well traveled. It has plenty of streams and water, a tantalizing glimpse of a huge waterfall and, at the top, an area which would take a whole day to explore. This would include visits to several mine areas including the old Blaine Mine perched high up at over 12,000 feet. It is also easily possible to link up with another trail leading southwards out of the Basin to a pass at 12,600 feet on the West side of Sneffels. Wildflowers abound right up into the Basin itself. The total round trip distance to the Basin is 6.5 miles. With the excursion to the pass it is 8 miles.

THE TRAIL

Drive north out of Ouray on Highway 550 to Ridgway. Turn left at Ridgway on Highway 62 and go west for 4.8 miles. Just before a newly built highway road bridge, turn left onto the East Dallas Creek National Forest Access Road. This is County Road 7. Follow direction signs for Uncompahgre National Forest access for 9 miles on a good gravel road. After 23.5 miles of driving form Ouray, cross the East Dallas Creek and half a mile farther on come to a junction with a sign pointing straight ahead for Blue Lakes Trailhead. Go straight ahead for 100 yards and find a parking place.

The trail starts virtually from the same place as the Blue Lakes Trail but it is important to set off on the right trail as it is not marked!

From the parking area walk south on the old jeep road for a few yards to a yellow metal swing gate. Proceed past the gate on the same road for another hundred yards to a Wilderness Information sign. At this point the Blue Lakes trail leads off to the right. Our trail carries on the old road and after another hundred yards, crosses the creek at an old bridge and proceeds up the hill to the left. After about .5 miles on this track you come to a sign at another junction which indicates Blaine Basin 2.5 miles back up to the right. Follow this sign and remain on the old unused jeep road for about 600 yards through spruce trees to a stream (Wilson Creek). Do not cross the stream here. Instead, go back 20 yards and look for a pile of rocks and a small trail going off to the right (west). This will take you to a better crossing point at a two-log bridge. Continue up the old jeep road on the other side and after about 50 yards bear sharp right back towards the mountain. Remain on the road and come to a pleasant opening lined with aspen trees. A little further on you come to the creek again. Cross on the wood logs and proceed again up the right hand side (west) of the creek going in a southerly direction towards the mountains. At this point it is worth keeping your eyes open just after crossing a small stream for a view of a waterfall which plunges down about 200 feet from a rock cliff to the right of the trail. Our own trail actually winds up to the left and comes out on top of this cliff. This is about 400 yards before arriving at a junction with a sign indicating Blaine Basin 1 mile, going left. (The trail going right takes you to the base of the waterfall). A little further on, after entering a (normally) dry creek, look for a less discernible trail about 30 yards up the creek on the right hand side. Do not proceed before locating this.

Head on up into a more open area and then keep right on

Blaine Basin — Sneffels is up to the right

a better defined trail. Come to another dry creek which has to be crossed and after .25 miles start to climb steeply up through the spruce again. After another half an hour the trail opens out by the creek and gives us our first fine view of the Basin and the North face of Sneffels. This is actually the lower Basin. The objective from here is to get to the top of the hill in front of you which appears to have been cleared of trees and then replanted with young spruce. The trail is not easy to find but the best way seems to be to keep left of the main creek and cross the smaller creek coming in from the left by walking upstream 30 yards. Then walk through the lush vegetation towards the right side of the small rock ridge ahead keeping the main creek just to your right. Here you should pick up the trail which winds up over the ridge and then zig-zags up the larger hill behind it. At the top of the hill the trail essentially ends at a beautiful rest place looking right into the main Basin. From this point it is possible to see the effects of the ice age glacial moraines and look straight up at the imposing but quite uninviting north side of Sneffels (14,150 feet). The mountain to the right is Blaine Peak and the highest peak round to the left (east of Sneffels) is Cirque Mountain (13,680 feet). The peak between Sneffels and Cirque is Kismet (13,694 feet).

Although this point is regarded as the destination for Blaine Basin, an interesting detour can be taken by looking up the grassy slope at the foot of Blaine Peak to the right where a trail can be clearly seen. To get to this, walk on 100 yards into the meadow towards Sneffels and then bear up right over grass and rocks to reach the visible trail. Then walk up it until it peters out and scramble up the scree and grassy rocky hill to the ledge at about 12,300 feet from where you can actually see another trail crossing the gully to the left (east) and eventually reaching the old Blaine Mine at the bottom left of Sneffels. (This excursion up and down takes at least an hour and is worth doing if time and energy permits).

To the left of the rest place, just across another small creek, are the remains of an old cabin and is a very pleasant camp site.

16. ICE LAKE

Elevation:	Start 9850 feet
	Top 12,257 feet
Time:	From Ouray to trailhead by car- 1 hour
	From trailhead to top 2.5 to 3 hours
	From top to bottom 1.5 hours
	Allow 5.5 to 6 hours for round trip (trail only)
Map:	USGS Topographical Ophir
Difficulty:	Difficult

GENERAL DESCRIPTION

It takes an hour by car to reach the trailhead but the extra time is well worth it. Without a doubt, this trail is a favorite of mine, as it combines all possible ingredients for a truly classic hike. Visually and scenically it is in the top league with streams, waterfalls, abundant wildflowers and meadows, great rock formations, alpine tundra and beautiful glacial lakes with magnificent backdrops of a mountain cirque reaching up over 13,500 feet.

The trail, which is a foot and horse trail, is fairly easy most of the way with two steep sections, one about half way up and one at the end. There are so many scenic rest stops that one does not have to make it to the top, although this would be a pity. The trail is well maintained and there is plenty of water for pets.

The round trip for the trail itself is a total of 7 miles.

THE TRAIL

Start Point: The trailhead is 26 miles from Ouray going south on Highway 550 towards Silverton. Go over Red Mountain Pass and after 21 miles (from Ouray) look for a sharp right turn marked "South Mineral Camp Ground." This turnoff is just before a 40 MPH sign and takes you on County Road 7 for 5 miles to the campground on a good gravel road. Just opposite the campground, on the right, there is a good parking area. Park here.

The trail from Ice Lake to Island Lake.

At the far end of the car park is an Ice Lake sign. This is the new trailhead; the old trailhead was 200 yards up the road going West and actually joins the main trail.

After about 15 minutes the trail crosses a creek. If you look up you can see a magnificent waterfall which later the trail traverses back towards and to a point where you can detour a few yards to the right to an old bridge across the face of the mountain. (Quite a spot for a photograph).

From here the trail winds up through a steep grassy slope filled with wildflowers. It then goes back into the spruce and aspen trees two or three more times.

After about 45 minutes of walking, note the old, wooden mine building and equipment on the left, and proceed on up through the meadow and back into the trees. After about another half an hour of switchbacks through the trees, the trail comes up over a ridge into the lower Ice Lake Basin at the 11,400 foot contour level. From here the trail meanders up through this beautiful basin at tree line with the lower Ice Lake on the left and a panorama of mountain views in front and on all sides. After about half a mile, look for the trail going up over the ridge in front to the left of the large smooth rock cliff.

Cross two streams coming down from a waterfall to the right and keep on the trail, now climbing again, towards the top of another waterfall to your left. Climb for 600 feet until you reach the level alpine tundra and keep on the trail until you see Ice Lake on the right.

It can be quite open and windy here and I have found the best spot to rest and have lunch is to the right of the lake where a stream exits down towards a waterfall. Here, protected by the stream bank, it is often sheltered and warm.

From any vantage point it is possible to view the huge cirque with U.S. Grant Peak (13,767 feet) directly North, around to Fuller Peak (13,761 feet) southwest.

If you wish to continue on the trail, which peters out, you can go south to Fuller Lake which is 300 ft. higher than Ice Lake but for a magnificent and well worth-it detour of 45 minutes, I recommend the simple climb up to Island Lake. This is reached by crossing the stream which comes out from the east side of the lake (described above as a resting place) and follow the trail up on your left (as you face down the big valley). The best crossing point on this stream is downstream about 200 yards, just before it topples over the waterfall. Just follow this little trail up the side of the mountain, looking back to see an original ore car still in place on a track outside an old mine towards a group of rocks. Follow on around a concave slope and then, keeping on the trail, stay on level ground for 300 yards to the lake which is below, with a small island in the middle. This lake's setting is absolutely magnificent and rewarding.

On the way back, after crossing the stream, keep straight on for a few yards to join to main Ice Lake Trail for the descent.

ჰჰ

17. COURTHOUSE MOUNTAIN

Elevation:	Start - 10,300 feet Top - 12,152 feet Round trip - approximately 4.5 miles
Time:	Ouray to start point by car - 1 hour 10 minutes Start point to top - 2.25 to 3 hours From top to bottom - 1.25 to 1.5 hours Allow 3.5 to 4.5 hours for round trip of trail itself Allow 6 to 7 hours for the total round trip from Ouray
Map:	USGS Topographical Courthouse Mountain
Difficulty:	Difficult

GENERAL DESCRIPTION

This is a beautiful trail in its own right with a magnificent drive to the trailhead. However, it does take over an hour to reach the start point and it should be stated that the trail itself, although starting off easy, becomes steeper and harder as it reaches the top with some scrambling and need to observe the correct way for the last 500 feet of elevation. I do not, therefore recommend this trail for the unfit, inexperienced or young children.

The views from the top are absolutely spectacular and offer the hiker as good a vantage point for 360° vision as any hike in this book. For sheer reward and accomplishment this hike is a ten.

THE TRAIL

The drive to the trailhead is 30.3 miles from Ouray and does not require a 4 WD or high clearance vehicle. Drive north to Ridgway on Highway 550 (10 miles). Continue on Highway 550 north for another 2 miles and turn right (east) onto County Road 10 marked Owl Creek Pass 13 miles. Keep on the main gravelled road for Owl Creek Pass even though County Road 10 becomes County Road 8. Cross Cow Creek and wind up past the sign for Uncompahgre National Forest and Road Number 858. Keep to the main road going up and eventually pass an open area in the aspen called Nate Creek Ditch. Very good views start to open up of Chimney Peak Rock (11,781 feet) on the right.

Continue up past the Owl Creek Pass summit of 10,114 feet which is 28.4 miles from Ouray and drive for one third of a mile to a junction just before the road starts down. Turn right here on "West Fork" and drive on past a couple of open areas and then past a place where side roads come in from the right and left and then to another larger open area on the left where you can see the creek Look for a clump of spruce trees at the end of this open area with a small parking area. This is exactly 1.6 miles in from the West Fork turn off and is our parking area. The trail, which is clearly marked "Courthouse Trail" starts right opposite off to the right hand side of the road.

Walk over the new little wooden bridge and head up gently on a well-defined trail through spruce trees. After about ten minutes or so the trail levels out and goes to the south passing a series of small drainages. It then starts to climb again, still under cover of the trees, and after about 45 minutes from the start, comes out on to a ridge with a large prominent rock boulder and a sign saying Big Blue Wilderness just to the left.

Our trail goes to the right and it is from this point on that the trail is not well marked and starts to get progressively more difficult. The main idea is to head right and hug the base of the ridged hill to the left and eventually come back up to the ridge in about a quarter of a mile. To do this, take the lower of the two trails going to the right of the rock, and keep more or less on the horizontal trail. For example, after 50 yards at a split in the trail, keep left and, a little further on, keep left again. After a few more minutes the trail turns up left to reach a little ridge from where you can get views down to the south and west. Go right here and follow just below the ridge to another vantage point on the left. Here you can see the fortress-like structure of Courthouse Mountain looming up in front of you.

After another few minutes the trail goes left and starts to climb more steeply towards the objective following the course

View from Courthouse Mountain looking east

of a steep meadowed gully. At first the trail stays to the left of the gully up through an area of downed trees, then climbs up (very steeply) through the center of it to another overlook which offers great views of the other side of Chimney Peak and, beyond it, to Silverjack Reservoir and beyond. Note the volcanic nature of the rock formations and excellent examples of erosion.

Continue on up the ridge towards the rock formations in front of you. At the top go right and then steep left up a rocky path to the right of a volcanic "wall." At the top of this steep path the hike turns into a scramble or easy climb. The best way up is to scramble up the series of rock "steps" in front of you to a small grassy knoll with a large single rock and a small cairn to its left. Follow up the grassy slope towards the talus looking for another cairn slightly to the left. From here, climb up towards another grassy area above and then, keeping a little to the left, reach a large pile of rocks. About 100 feet above this it should be possible to relocate a trail of sorts at another cairn which goes diagonally left across another grassy area just below the rock ridge above. At the top left hand side of this the trail goes up through a little chimney and then heads steeply up the final grassy ridge for 200 feet to the top.

It can be very exposed and windy on top but the views are magnificent. To the west, on the horizon can be seen the La Sal Mountains and the Henries in Utah, to their left is the beautiful expanse of the Sneffels Range extending all the way round to Ouray. To the south is the Amphitheater, Dexter Creek and the Big Blue Wilderness while over to the east there are wonderful views of the West and Middle Forks of the Cimarrons with Dunsinane Mountain (12,742 feet) right opposite and the large feature of Sheep Mountain (13,168) beyond. To the north, beyond Chimney Peak is Ridgway, Montrose, Delta, Paonia area and Grand Mesa.

18. MOUNT ABRAMS

Elevation:	Start - 11,600 feet
	Top - 12,801 feet (The climb itself entails a good deal more than this elevation gain indicates)
Time:	From Ouray to trailhead by vehicle - 30 minutes
	From trailhead to top - 2.5 to 3 hours
	From top to bottom - 1.5 hours
	Allow 5 hours for round trip (trail itself)
Map:	USGS Topographical Ironton
Difficulty:	Difficult

GENERAL DESCRIPTION

If there is one mountain that everybody in Ouray would call their own it is Mount Abrams. As you drive into Ouray from the north or enjoy the hot springs water of the pool it is the classically beautiful pyramid-shaped mountain dominating the Southern panorama. Actually Mount Abrams is but one of many peaks on the huge Brown Mountain ridge but it is the most Northerly and obviously deserves its own name.

Climbing it is quite a formidable task. There is no actual trail but, with good instructions, the mountain can be climbed safely without too much trouble. Wildflowers abound.

Conventionally, there is a hard way and an easy way. Having done both more than once this guide will concentrate on the easier route, which requires a vehicle with high clearance to drive up to a start point of 11,600 feet, but refer briefly to the harder way as it is possible to combine both into a loop (for which two vehicles would be necessary). In both cases, there is a considerable amount of steep uphill plod up grassy tundra and depending on paths taken, there can be rock, scree, and a little rough terrain. However, it is certainly not technical. Our recommended route provides some of the finest ridge walking possible and offers views which compare with any hike in the state.

There is very little water and none whatsoever after leaving the gulches. It can also be very windy, quite cold and exposed on the top ridge.

The round trip, as described here, is about four and a half miles.

THE TRAIL

Drive south on Highway 550 towards Red Mountain Pass. As you do so Mount Abrams forms a perfect triangle in front of you. Drive past the snowshed and the first set of switchbacks to where the road starts to flatten out. This is the six mile point from Ouray. Look for a single stone building on the left (the old Saint Germain Foundation). Behind this to the left there is a definite clearing with trees on either side of it leading up into a gulch. For the hard way up or to complete a loop this is where to park a vehicle. The hard route leaves the clearing at the stream and switchbacks up left (north) of the gulch through the aspen and spruce keeping well left of the steep rock formation and then leads freely straight up the mountainside past the tree-line towards a small rock escarpment where you should stay to the right and then wind back on to the summit. This is a hard slog and climbs 3200 feet so count on it being exhausting. [If the plan is to do the loop then one vehicle should be parked near the Saint Germain Foundation building.]

The route takes us another 1.4 miles (7.4 miles from Ouray) to the large square-looking mine tailings on the left. Turn off the highway to the left just as you come to the tailings. There should be a sign saying Corkscrew Gulch and Brown Mountain.

After driving along the side of the tailings a junction is reached. Turn left here for Brown Mountain and immediately cross a stream staying on the relatively good road. From this point on keep to the main road which is always ascending. Come to some interesting mine buildings passing a rough spot in the road and continue on up switchbacking for about 2 miles after which it starts to open out a little and then re-enters trees. After another half a mile the road comes to a definite T-junction with a small pond right in front of you. Go left here and drive

Mount Abrams from just north of Ouray

on up for about 300 yards to a point where it goes down to a creek or cuts back up to the right. Park here.

As you get out and look North towards the Brown Mountain ridge there are actually three ways to go — all leading eventually to the same place, which is the ridge at the top of and slightly to the left of the gulch in front of you (Brooklyn Gulch). Some people prefer to walk up the jeep road which goes back up to the right and which, after 100 yards, cuts back towards the gulch. After it cuts back, look for a pile of rock scree with a post stuck in it. Immediately after this, start climbing up the slope towards a cluster of small spruce. This is actually a small trail which traverses up to meet the gulch 300 feet higher up. Alternatively, if you do not take this trail, but instead, carry on walking the jeep track to the gulch, you will see a small trail crossing the creek and heading up left to another small clump of trees on the other side of the creek. After reaching these trees, bear right and head up the left side of the gulch.

Finally (and it really makes no difference) one can just climb up the path of the gulch! In all three cases the objective is to hit the ridge line just left of the gulch past a small stand of vegetation and just to the right of a rocky outcrop. There is a

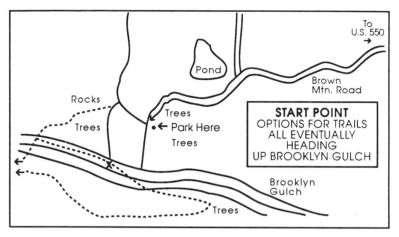

MT. ABRAMS - Start Point options.

tendency to want to go up diagonally to the left but this will lead you into the path of large areas of scree and some unattractive ground. If you hit the ridge at the saddle above the gulch where you can see down the other side, you should see an indistinct trail coming in from the right. Turn left on this trail and follow it as far as you can but where it descends to the left, keep on the ridge. It should have taken about an hour to reach this point.

The roads that can be seen on the other side are Engineer Pass going east and Poughkeepsie Gulch following the ridge line south. To the West is the giant feature of Hayden Mountain with the Million Dollar Highway running south to Red Mountain Pass.

I prefer to keep on the ridge for the next half a mile mainly because of the views but as long as you keep going north towards the farthest peak which is Abrams it is okay. At this point Abrams appears to be the other side of a horrendous ravine like obstacle but don't worry: it's not that bad!

A little later on you may notice a more definite looking trail down to the right. Stay on this trail until you come to a chalky white-colored saddle. The trail heads up gently to the right for 200 yards to an overlook from where you can see the trail pick up again on the far side. Traverse round left to meet the trail again. Usually the ridge to this point has taken another hour.

Hwy. 550 from Mt. Abrams looking south towards Red Mtn. Pass

Proceed to the next large rock outcrop. Go left and pick up the trail again for 100 yards. At the little knoll, head up diagonally to the right for a 200 foot elevation gain until you come to the top of the ridge again. Depending on where you hit it, look north towards Ouray to reach a four foot high cairn with a marker on it. This is the summit! From the cairn it is possible to get a good view of two local fourteeners, Uncompahgre Peak out on the north east skyline and Mount Sneffels directly to the West just to the right of the Potosi Peak feature. Meanwhile the gem of the Rockies nestled below provides a superb opportunity to capture the atmosphere of Ouray from this great vantage point.

To return I suggest the same route although it is possible to cut down diagonally to the right going south but this entails a lot of scree and rock hiking.

For those wanting to do the loop the 'vertical' descent can be achieved by getting to a point from where you can see the Saint Germain Foundation building and heading on down. However, it is definitely easier to stay well to the right of the big gulch (Hendrick Gulch) to avoid the steep cliff-like formations below the Lucky Twenty Mine at the 10,600 feet level. If you are fortunate it is sometimes possible to link up with the old pack trail which starts at the tree line at about 11,300 feet about 400 yards to the north of the gulch. Whatever the route selected to come down, this way is strenuous and extra time should be allowed.

19. MOUNT HAYDEN

Elevation:	Start - 9400 feet from trailhead or 8,600 feet from road
	Top - 12,578 feet
Time:	Ouray to start point (by vehicle) - 15 to 20 minutes
	Start to top - 3 to 4 hours
	Top to bottom - 2 hours
	Total round trip - 6 to 7 hours for the trail itself (add one hour if walking up to the trailhead from main road)
Map:	USGS Topographical Ironton and Ouray
Difficulty:	Difficult

GENERAL DESCRIPTION

To be honest it was only after a little soul-searching that I gave-in to the idea that this trail should be included with all the others. The reason for holding back was purely selfish. Apart from being my own personal favorite, it starts virtually from our own doorstep but is little known, unmarked and with a trailhead that is difficult to locate, unless you know exactly where to go. However, on the plus side, this trail is amongst the finest anywhere because of its pristine quality. It is very much a "destination" trail and is not the easiest. In fact some would call it more of a climb than a hike, and the descent can be particularly hard on the knees and is quite slippery even with good hiking boots. Nevertheless it is literally a "peak experience" and for those who really want to climb a mountain from whose top the beauty of the views surpass nearly everything else in the area, this is a must.

The trail itself varies from pleasant, soft, underfoot, to much uphill rocky scree and about a thousand feet of steep tundra with a little rock scrambling on top. There is little or no water on the trail and in terms of effort it is definitely one of the more strenuous and probably not suitable for inexperienced

Looking south towards the easternmost summit of the Hayden group of peaks (the top point is the objective)

hikers or those who are out of shape. To get to the trailhead requires either four-wheel drive or a vehicle with high clearance, although one can walk up the mile long vehicle road to the trailhead from a good parking spot in about twenty-five minutes.

THE TRAIL

To get to the trailhead drive South out of Ouray and take the first turn to the right off of the second switchback onto County Road 361 leading to Camp Bird Mine and Yankee Boy Basin. Drive up the road from the turn off for about 1.7 miles looking for a white polyvinyl vent pipe sticking out of the bank on the left side of the road. Just past this is a definite fork to the left where there are usually a couple of real estate signs. Turn left here and immediately bear left again. Do not follow the horizontal drive parallel to the creek which goes to private residences but head, instead, up the hill. Incidentally, if you miss this turn off and get to the bridge on the County Road 361 you have gone a quarter of a mile too far!

The first 300 yards or so of the road to the trailhead is

extremely rough and definitely requires 4-wheel dirve or high clearance. After that the road gets easier and continues for exactly a mile gaining about 800 feet in elevation. However, after about half a mile there is a junction and here your must keep straight on and not bear left. At the one mile point there is another junction and here you should go left passing a small old shed-like building. Park 50 yards above this shed on the side.

As a little detour here, one can walk on past this turn off at the shed for a short distance, keeping to the main vehicle track, to the old Cutler Mine (for which the road was built).

Our trail starts out from where the vehicle should be parked going up to the right, through heavy spruce and aspen on a relatively steep but shaded path for about 15 minutes and then levels out before gaining more elevation.

After another 15 minutes or so the trail opens out into Squaw Gulch where it becomes rocky underfoot -- with interesting pinnacle formations up to the right. After 300 yards the trail begins to switchback steeply up the narrow valley side towards the mine tailings at the top of the valley. (It is this section that many people have a problem with on the descent!) From here there are great views looking across Canyon Creek to Weehawken Creek, Alpine Mine Overlook and Angel Creek, and the foliage and wildflowers are particularly lush and colorful. After about an hour from the start, the trail crosses the mine tailings and goes to the right, back into the spruce. This small area of comparatively level walking is at the 10,800 contour line and if you look back down to the right it is just possible to catch a glimpse of Ouray before the trail heads back southward.

Ten minutes later the trail breaks out onto a ridge and turns left. This is a perfect rest spot and provides superb views up towards Camp Bird and the 13,000 foot high San Sofia Ridge which makes the boundary between Ouray and San Miguel County. But more importantly, up to the left, we see our first real view of our objective -- the superbly proportioned and majestic northeast shoulder of Hayden Mountain.

The trail proceeds through healthy aspen stands up a steep grassy slope, switchbacking up to the ridge line and then back

View from Mt. Hayden looking east up Bear Creek
(to left) and Engineer Pass Road (to right)

into spruce which takes us to the forested saddle to the left of
the mountain.

A little further on the trail comes to a very small grassy
meadow and appears to peter out. Go on through the opening
between two fallen trees and then bear right where the trail
picks up again. From here it climbs steeply, again in spruce.
Keep on the main trail just after reentering the spruce and do
not go left, which is a deer trail. Just past this, observant hikers
will notice a trail blaze marker on a tree to the right where the
trail now does switchback up to the left. You can now follow
other old trail blaze signs until you come out into the open on
the saddle. If you keep walking for another 100 yards to the
overlook, which provides excellent views down to the Million
Dollar Highway, this also serves as another suitable rest place,
which for reference, is about two thirds in time, to the summit
with still over a thousand feet to go.

From here it is pretty well every man or woman for
himself/herself! At our rest point you will notice a small pit in
the ground resembling a dry water hole with a cairn (pile of
rocks) by the side of it. Just above this, heading up into the

spruce a less discernible trail can be seen, complete with trail blaze marks. Take this trail as far as you can and then head up through the path of least resistance to the tree line, above which can be seen the triangular shape of the objective. I have found that the old trail does go up through the trees to a "T" and then appears to end. My recommendation is to bear left here and keep climbing up towards the left to the tree line. It really does not matter much at this point because all routes will eventually come out onto the grassy steep mountainside. At the tree line, the easiest route seems to be to head for a clump of small weathered spruce slightly to the right and then on up to another bush-like spruce (which is the highest tree on the mountain) on the ridge to the left. From here I suggest keeping to the left of the rocky outcrops, which serve as homes for several families of ptarmigans, until you come to a sort of saddle on the left, just below the final summit formation. Here, one can either go left and traverse across and up the grassy tundra to the Hayden Ridge or just carry on up as far as the grass leads and scramble up the rock and scree for the final two hundred feet.

At the top there is (usually) a white marker post marking the peak at 12,578 feet and there is plenty of room for relaxing and intake of calories and liquid.

The views provide an exquisite reward for this 3,200 foot climb. To the west, the road up into Yankee Boy Basin can be clearly seen. To its right, in the foreground, is the 13,786 foot Potosi Peak with Cirque and Teakettle just to its right. Mount Sneffels at 14,150 feet is the darker, less noticeable peak jotting up just to the right of and behind Potosi. The other highly visible features a little to the east of these mountains are Mt. Ridgway and Whitehouse with Twin Peaks way down there to the right and the unmistakable shape of Courthouse Mountain rising up behind Dexter Creek. Looking over the ridge to the south, there are clear views of the Engineer Pass Road, Bear Creek, Mount Abrams and Red Mountain.

If time permits, it is worth continuing along the Hayden Ridge although one needs to be careful in places. The next Peak is 12,687 feet and the other peaks, all of which compose Hayden Mountain are 12,864 feet and 13,200 feet respectively. However, after reaching the next peak on the ridge line the terrain becomes dangerous and extreme caution is urged. Similarly, although it is possible to descend down the southeast side of the mountain towards Ironton, I do not recommend this without a guide as some of the rock and scree slopes above the treeline are unstable and there is no trail at all for the first 2000 feet of elevation loss.

20. MOUNT SNEFFELS

Elevation:	Start point (recommended) 11,760 feet
	Start point (alternative) 11,440 feet
	Start point (2-wheel drive) 11,000 feet approx.
	Top 14,150 feet
	Elevation gain 2,390 + (depending on start point)
Time:	Ouray to start point - 35 to 45 minutes (by vehicle)
	Start point (recommended) to Top - 2 to 3 hours
	Top to bottom - 1.5 to 2 hours
	Round-trip - Allow 4.5 to 6 hours (trail itself)
Map:	USGS Topographical Ouray, Ironton, and Telluride
Difficulty:	Difficult

GENERAL DESCRIPTION

This is our local fourteener. The summit is actually 14,150 feet and the name derives from the Icelandic mountain called Mt. Sneffels in the early novel "A Journey to the Center of the Earth" by Jules Verne.

The climb is mainly on scree and talus (rock boulders) with some scrambling near the top. The trail round-trip is about 4 miles but remember that the elevations and angle of the climb combined with possible adverse weather conditions make this a longer hike than one thinks. In fact for all practical purposes it should be considered a non-technical climb. Conditions can vary tremendously and it is not unusual to encounter snow, sleet, rain, mist, and cold at any time of the year. Before July there can still be quite a lot of snow in the top couloir and this snow can start accumulating again by the end of August.

The main criteria for making this hike successful is to know the correct route and to start early, otherwise it can be danger-

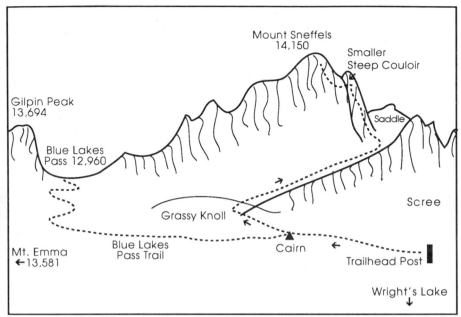

SNEFFELS TRAIL - From the Main Trailhead Post

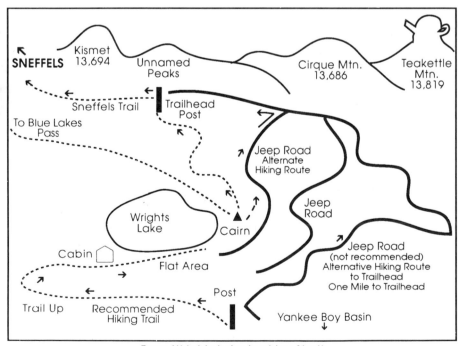

From Wrights Lake Looking North

ous and costly in time and energy. Unfortunately it seems that a lot of people literally start to climb the wrong mountain or never even get to know exactly which mountain is Sneffels. The descriptions written here will therefore be as explanatory as possible in order to avoid misunderstandings. Good advice involves taking it slowly and carrying warm weather equipment. Sneakers are apt to get wet and cold, especially if snow exists in the couloir. Another major factor in calculating times is the selected start point. Although some 2-wheel drive vehicles can make it, a 4-wheel drive or vehicle with high clearance is necessary to get to the best start point, otherwise another 2 miles of walking, each way, is required. Notwithstanding the above, the drive up through Yankee Boy Basin from Ouray to the start point is an experience in itself and boasts some of the finest wildflower and mountain scenery in the entire area.

THE TRAIL

To get to the various start points, take Highway 550 south out of Ouray (the Red Mountain Pass Road) and turn right after the first switchback on County Road 361, following signs to Camp Bird, Yankee Boy Basin and Imogene Pass. Proceed up this good gravel road for 5.5 miles until you can see the huge Camp Bird Mine complex down to the left. Here, go right on the road signed for Imogene and Yankee Boy Basin. After half a mile or so drive under the rock overhang and just under a mile later look for the small sign indicating the Imogene Pass Road going off to the left. Do not take this left turn, but continue up the main road past an old mine and a working mine to a sign giving information about the old town of Sneffels. Keep on the main road past the great wooden ruins of the old Atlas Mill on the other side of the creek. A little further on there is a fork with the road to Governor Basin going down to the left and Yankee Boy Basin up to the right. Proceed right on the Yankee Boy Basin road but from this point onwards beware of the ruts and unevenness of the road. Low clearance vehicles are likely to experience (expensive) trouble! After another half a mile you can see the beautiful twin falls waterfall on the left. This is the

*Taken from above Wrights Lake, Sneffels is the peak in
the distance poking up into the vapor trail.
The main couloir can be seen going up to the right by the small
snowfield halfway up and to the left in this picture.*

site for many summer weddings and has also been used by
Coors for their beer commercials. Bear in mind, however, that
at this point you cannot really see Sneffels and the mountain
you think is Sneffels is really a peak of 13,694 feet called Kismet.
After another half a mile of driving into Yankee Boy Basin itself
(about 8.4 miles from Ouray), a decision should be made to park
here (in the vicinity of a new restroom facility provided by the
city of Ouray) or to proceed on across the stream ahead and up
the jeep road going diagonally up the side of the hill in front of
you. If so keep right after 100 yards and drive on over various
puddles to the base of the hill by a stream. Do not take the fork
to the right at the stream.

If you decide to drive up the steep hill, there is a small
parking place for about 4 vehicles on the right about 400 yards
up just before a steep switchback to the right. At this point is a
stout post in the ground indicating a hiking trail going straight
ahead. This is my recommendation for parking and starting the
hike. Alternatively (and only for four-wheelers with experience
and high clearance) one can go up the switchback to the right

and drive up through the potholes and nasty deep rocky ridges to arrive, after a mile, to a parking area on the tundra next to a sign marker. I do not recommend this however.

Now, I am going to give two ways of starting the climb, both of which should end up at the same place and both assume starting from my recommended start point — at the top of the jeep road, which is approximately 9.5 miles from Ouray.

The first, (and I think best) method is to walk up the well defined trail from the post for about 20 minutes to a small lake called Wrights Lake (12,200 feet) with a building on the left near side which is now used by the Ouray Mountain Rescue Team. The view from the trail up to the lake looking back down into Yankee Boy Basin is one of the best available, especially when the wildflowers are in bloom in July and early August. From the lake, keeping the cabin on the left go around slightly to the right where there is a junction of jeep roads. With your eye, follow up the path of the jeep road on the left (the one nearest the lake) and when you loose sight of it on the near horizon, look left about 300 yards at the same elevation and identify a post in the ground. This post, which is about 600 yards from the lake is our best trail head. Either go up the jeep road and bear left or just walk up to the post cross-country. There may even be a vehicle or two parked there.

The second method by which this post can be reached is to walk up the jeep road which switchbacks sharply to the right from our original start point. Carry on this very bad road until it comes out on top, above and to the right of the lake, and follow it around to the trailhead post. (If you do this you'll see why I did not recommend it for vehicles).

To further complicate matters, back at the lake, you can see a cairn (pile of rocks) on the far right side of the lake with a trail heading off up to the left towards the gravelly cliff cutting the skyline to the west. This is considered to be the old Blue Lakes Pass Trail and if you look again at the gravelly cliff you will see a trail zig-zagging its way up over the top. Admittedly one could take this trail part of the way and look for where it eventually meets our trail but I still prefer my original recommendation! At any rate the objective is to head west over the

The final scramble to the top looking back to the east

grassy and rocky surface until you see the very large couloir (gully) opening out and going up to the right. The mountain (Sneffels) is the peak to the left of the couloir as you go up.

At the trailhead post, mentioned previously, there should be a clearly marked sign which says Lower Blue Lakes 3.5 miles, East Dallas Creek 7 miles. Take this trail, which goes mainly on the flat over rocks for about half a mile to the west and then, at another cairn, splits. The left fork meets the other trail coming up from Wrights Lake and traverses up the steep wall in front to the top of Blue Lakes Pass at 12,960 feet. The right fork, which is the one we want, winds up for a short distance over a grassy slope, which houses a family of almost tame marmots, and then heads right (north) up the large couloir for some 800 feet to a saddle at the top. For safety reasons it is best to keep to the middle of this couloir and definitely not try to undertake any so-called short cuts by going up to the left which is where the summit is but which, at this point, you cannot properly see. Take it slowly up the couloir. Some people prefer the gravelly zig-zag trail and other prefer the more stable rock. In any case, just head up for the saddle, which is about 13,500 feet and looks down the other side to Blaine Basin. Hiking time to this point should be 1.5 to 2 hours.

From here, another, narrower and shorter couloir can be seen going up to the left (west). Proceed up this carefully. The most used route (at the time of writing) is on the left of this couloir but, again, some prefer just scrambling up the rock talus. About 300 feet further up it is likely that snow will be encountered. This often remains in the gully all year, but some years it remains just on the right side. Go up it slowly making sure that one foothold is secure before moving again. For some, keeping to the right against the rock wall will be easier.

At the top of the snow area you can now see another smaller saddle. Just before this saddle on the left, about 30 feet down from the saddle, is a small V-shaped notch in the rock. This little notch or chimney is our trail. Look for a wedged rock at the bottom for a foothold and just up to the right are several good handholds. After negotiating this little obstacle, keep right on a recognizably trodden trail and head up towards two vertical rocks with a small rock wedged between them. When you reach this point, bear left and scramble the last fifty feet to the summit where you can find a plastic cylinder with paper in it to sign your name.

From the top are outstanding views of every mountain in the area including, to the far east, another fourteener, Uncompahgre Peak. Below to the west are the upper and lower Blue Lakes. To the south are the upper slopes of the Telluride Ski Area and to the northeast is Ridgway, the Dallas Reservoir (Dutch Charlie), Montrose and, in the distance, Grand Mesa.

Caution: Descend the same way. If connecting with the Dallas Creek / Blue Lakes Trail, go back down the two couloirs to the trail junction point where the cairn is and then bear right up Blue Lakes Pass. Lastly, for best results, I strongly recommend starting early. It really is worth it to plan leaving Ouray by 7 AM in order to get the most beneficial experience and be off the mountain top by noon.

🚶🚶

🚶 Hiking Notes

ABOUT THE AUTHOR

Kelvin Kent was born and brought up on the Island of Jersey in the British Channel Islands. After leaving school he worked in London for three years and was later drafted into the British Military where he became commissioned into the Royal Corps of Signals. After declining a good offer to return to civilian life he served for another sixteen years around the world including over six years with the Gurkha Troops from Nepal. Later, as a Company Commander at the Royal Military Academy at Sandhurst, he was in charge of Army Adventure Training.

In 1976 he retired from the British Army as a major and moved to the United States.

He has hiked extensively in many countries and has been a member of several expeditions in Europe, Asia, Africa and South America. He has also participated in two Himalayan mountaineering expeditions with the Chris Bonington team.

He is currently the owner of Montrose Decorating Center in Montrose and, together with his wife Becky Lindsay DDS, spends a good portion of the year in the Ouray area where they have a cabin on the Camp Bird Mine Road.

Atop Mt. Hayden - Kelvin, Becky, Angie and Melanie

⋈ HIKING NOTES

♨ HIKING NOTES